Towards a New Concept of the Political

I0129003

This book addresses the current crisis of democratic politics and its phase of 'interregnum' – in which the past finds it hard to die and the future finds it difficult to be born – by proposing a radical redefinition of the concept of the Political.

Drawing on the thoughts of Antonio Gramsci and Walter Benjamin among others, it explores the meaning of the *lemma auctoritas* – the opposition between authority and power – and offers a comparison of the Frankfurt School's radical critique of power with Georges Bataille's critique of political economy and consumerist productivism, demonstrating how the two ultimately converge. Based on an ontology of the present that is critical of 'identity obsession' and advances instead a universalism of difference, the author proposes a new understanding of politics founded not on 'vertical' domination but on a 'horizontal' recomposition of subjectivities, allowing interaction and acting-in-common between different forms of life.

This book will therefore appeal to scholars of social and political theory.

Giacomo Marramao is Emeritus Professor of Philosophy at the Roma Tre University, Italy. He is also a member of the Honor Committee of the Collège International de Philosophie in Paris, France, and has been the recipient of numerous academic awards. His research explores theoretical and political philosophy, with particular emphasis on questions of power, hegemony, modernity, and time. He is the author of numerous books, several of which have been translated into various languages, including *The Passage West: Philosophy After the Age of the Nation State* (2012), *Against Power: For an Overhaul of Critical Theory* (2016), and *The Bewitched World of Capital: Methods, Theory, Politics* (2023).

Critiques and Alternatives to Capitalism
Series editor: **Marcello Musto**, *Professor of Sociological Theory*,
York University, Canada

This series publishes scholarly works on critiques and alternatives to capitalism, spanning a number of subject matters, political perspectives, and geographical areas. It welcomes monographs and edited volumes in the fields of sociology, social and political theory, and heterodox political economy, whose main areas of focus are the problems of capitalist society and its mode of production, alternatives to capitalism that address contemporary social issues, and nineteenth and twentieth centuries' anti-capitalist ideas and practical experiments.

Welcoming new perspectives on a wide range of themes, it seeks to explore alternative social-economic systems, critical theories of capitalism, social classes and inequality, public/private ownership and new contours of 'the commons', economic and financial crises, ecology, globalization, migration and citizenship, gender oppression, alienation, and cultural critique. The result is an eclectic, but focused and informative, series that provides original investigations, inspires significant conversations for today, and appeals to a diverse international audience.

Overcoming Exploitation and Externalization
An Intersectional Theory of Hegemony and Transformation
Friederike Habermann

The Commons
A Force in the Socio-Ecological Transition to Postcapitalism
César Rendueles

Heidegger in the Face of the Environmental Question
The Immanence of Life
Enrique Leff

Towards a New Concept of the Political
A Defence of Universalism and Difference
Giacomo Marramao

For more information about this series, please visit: www.routledge.com/Critiques-and-Alternatives-to-Capitalism/book-series/CAATC

Towards a New Concept of the Political

A Defence of Universalism and Difference

Giacomo Marramao

With an Afterword by Hayden White

Routledge
Taylor & Francis Group

LONDON AND NEW YORK

First published 2024
by Routledge
4 Park Square, Milton Park, Abingdon, Oxon OX14 4RN

and by Routledge
605 Third Avenue, New York, NY 10158

*Routledge is an imprint of the Taylor & Francis Group, an
informa business*

© 2024 Giacomo Marramao

The right of Giacomo Marramao to be identified as author of
this work has been asserted in accordance with sections 77
and 78 of the Copyright, Designs and Patents Act 1988.

British Library Cataloguing-in-Publication Data
A catalogue record for this book is available from the British Library

ISBN: 9781032612478 (hbk)
ISBN: 9781032632834 (pbk)
ISBN: 9781032632827 (ebk)

DOI: 10.4324/9781032632827

Typeset in Times New Roman
by Deanta Global Publishing Services, Chennai, India

Contents

Prologue

A famous sentence by Hegel assigned philosophy the task of understanding its own time with thought, bringing it back to the concept.

With our globalized hyper-modernity, the efficacy – even symbolic – of the State, an artificial organism for which Hobbes had chosen the 'monstrous' emblem of the biblical Leviathan, has been exhausted. The breaking of the political monotheism that elected it to the maximum earthly power, exclusive source of sovereignty and law, has given new strength to indirect powers of an economic and religious type and has brought the modern antinomy between the two principles of identity and difference to the fore. The after which we have seen distinctly looming at the advent of the new millennium now replaces its time mark with a spatial mark. Only a thought of space, of heterogeneous and incompressible contiguity, is in fact up to our present and its urgencies: taking leave of a logic of identity and restoring to politics the ability to give meaning to collective action.

According to the author of the present book, this responsibility to conceptualize the present, characteristic of the modern era, cannot today be delegated to other forms of knowledge, and even less transferable to those who claim to be the custodians of the resources of meaning.

However, the Hegelian precept must be redefined outside of privileged statutes and logics of supremacy: if responsibility – as taught by the late Jacques Derrida – means *responding to* rather than *responding of*, responding to someone rather than responding of something, then letting yourself be challenged by the present it involves intensifying the dialogical tenor of reflection and otherwise dislocating as a questioner.

And it is from a new, and destabilizing, optical vertex that the various chapters of this book look at the uneven transitions and misunderstandings of globalization, at its identity rigidities and temporal pathologies, at its false alternatives (universalism or particularism, normativism or relativism) and to its immovable polarities (first of all, East/West).

At the same time indispensable and inadequate, the universalistic categories of law and *humanitas* regain strength only when they are brought into tension with the emotional experiences of value and the rhetoric at work in the story of oneself, to which a conceptual statute must be restored.

Move in the perspective of redefining politics in an uncertain and 'unmentionable' present, marked by uncertainties and conflicts, oscillating between fear and hope, in a sort of interregnum between the no-longer than an old time who is slow to die and the not-yet of a young time who is struggling to be born, today means going through a series of neuralgic nodes that invest both the structure and the subjects:

- from the concept of 'interregnum' understood as a divorce between power and authority to the paradigm of delegitimization as a peculiar feature of the populist syndrome;
- from the 'state of exception' in the confrontation between Carl Schmitt and Walter Benjamin to the sovereignty of unproductive expenditure of Georges Bataille and the Parisian Collège de Sociologie;
- from an increasingly multipolar and 'intersectional' globalization, composed of 'multiple modernities' and populated by a variety of 'Easts' and 'Wests' to a Theatrum Mundi increasingly hegemonized by continent-states such as the USA, China, India, and Russia.

In the face of this scenario, the book proposes an ontology of the present based on the radical critique of every form of 'identity obsession' and on the thesis of a *universalism of difference* and a *politics of translation* capable of establishing a constant interaction between the various 'forms of life'.

A concept of the Political suitable for today's world can only be constructed by keeping together global and local, the destiny of the planet and the dimension of singularity with its irreducible elements, and not starting from identity in its various community, state, ethnic, or linguistic configurations.

It is therefore necessary to introduce a clear *line of demarcation between conflict and war*: war is not only an inhuman and non-humanizable event but, above all, the most brutal device for neutralizing the regenerating symbolic potential of conflict.

Let us, therefore, return – to enter one of the crucial passages of this book – to Walter Benjamin's comparison with Carl Schmitt on the theme of the 'state of exception'. They are very different positions, even politically antagonistic, although they are closely related conceptually. However, it is an example of how the tension towards an integral concept of the Political can be released from a paradigmatic antithesis, which includes at the same time the dimensions of praxis and of *kairòs*, of *politics as a process* and of *politics as an event*.

The cardinal virtue of politics lies entirely in the ability to grasp the 'signs of the times': exactly in the expression that we find in Matthew's Gospel. But here attention should be paid to the terms present in the sentence.

In the Greek version, Matthew does not use the term *chrónos* to denote time but *kairós*: the 'opportune time', the 'due time' capable of taking into account the 'tempers', of a variable conjunction of elements similar to that of the atmospheric weather. 'Signs of the times' in Greek is *sēmeia tōn kairōn*: thus indicating not the serial and undifferentiated time of measurement, but the qualitative time of the conjuncture, of kairós.

In short, the linear, neutral time of chronological succession does not emit signals to be deciphered. Only the qualitative time of the conjuncture, of the climate, awaits to be decoded.

But let's read the entire passage: 'Today it's stormy, because the sky is dark red. So you know how to interpret the appearance of the sky and you are not able to interpret the signs of the times (*sēmeia tōn kairōn*)?' (Mt. 16,3).

Today as yesterday, today more than yesterday, the concept of the Political cannot disregard the categorical imperative to interpret the 'signs of the times'.

Giacomo Marramao
Florence-Rome, April–May 2023

1 Our Present as an Interregnum

The Metaphor of the Interregnum

'Interregnum' here serves as a metaphor for the suspended time that characterizes our present. The term was 'originally used to denote a time-lag separating the death of one royal sovereign from the enthronement of the successor'. This meaning was then transposed and applied to a stalemate situation between the 'no longer' of the old, dying order and the 'not yet' of a new order struggling to come into being.

The primary stage for this transfer, which is widely referred to yet little understood in its actual meaning, is represented by a compelling reflection that Antonio Gramsci provides in his *Prison Notebooks*:

> That aspect of the modern crisis which is bemoaned as a 'wave of materialism' is related to what is called the 'crisis of authority'. If the ruling class has lost its consensus, i.e. is no longer 'leading' but only 'dominant', exercizing coercive force alone, this means precisely that the great masses have become detached from their traditional ideologies, and no longer believe what they used to believe previously, etc. The crisis consists precisely in the fact that the old is dying and the new cannot be born; in this interregnum a great variety of morbid symptoms appear. N.B. this paragraph should be completed by some observations which I made on the so-called 'problem of the younger generation' – a problem caused by the 'crisis of authority' of the old generations in power, and by the mechanical impediment that has been imposed on those who could exercise hegemony, which prevents them from carrying out their mission. The problem is the following: can a rift between popular masses and ruling ideologies as serious as that which emerged after the war be 'cured' by the simple exercise of force, preventing the new ideologies from imposing themselves? Will the interregnum, the crisis whose historically normal solution is blocked in this way, necessarily be resolved in favour of a restoration of the old? Given the character of the ideologies, that can be ruled out – yet not in an absolute sense. [1]

DOI: 10.4324/9781032632827-1

Renowned commentators (especially historians, but also some philosophers) have been captivated by the most evocative expressions used in this passage, such as the reference to the 'morbid symptoms' manifesting themselves in this stagnant backwash in the movement of history. However, they have over-looked the most significant and meaningful core of Gramsci's reflection: the idea of the 'crisis of authority' of a power no longer capable of 'leading' but only of 'dominating'. Yet this is a crucial insight: it is as though Gramsci had, on the unstable ridge of an interlude in the dynamics of history, laid the foundations for a 'post-hegemonic' view through this thought, opening up a field of tension between power and authority. I will be focusing on this motif in the final pages of this introductory section. For the time being, it is important not to lose sight of the position of the interregnum within a diagnostic category for the present that is marked by the pair of elements called the 'wave of materialism' and 'crisis of authority'. The interregnum, then, does not depend on a crisis of apparatuses and structures but rather on a crisis that is at once cultural and systemic, and in which the objective element and the subjective entail each other, leading to the survival of a power without authority: a power reduced to mere 'domination'.

Zygmunt Bauman explicitly latches onto this text by Gramsci in a 2012 essay with an almost programmatic title: 'Times of Interregnum'.[2] Quite reasonably, he draws inspiration from Gramsci's diagnosis in order to bring it up to date in relation to the conditions of our time, marked by the loss of the modern triad of State–Territory–Sovereignty:

> The old order founded until recently on a similarly 'triune' principle of territory, state, and nation as the key to the planetary distribution of sovereignty, and on power wedded seemingly forever to the politics of the territorial nation-state as its sole operating agency, is by now dying. Sovereignty is no longer glued to either of the elements of the triune principle and entities; at the utmost, it is tied to them but loosely and in portions much reduced in size and contents. The allegedly unbreakable marriage of power and politics is, however, ending in separation with a prospect of divorce.[3]

What seems problematic, instead, is the picture he draws of the new global stage:

> Sovereignty is nowadays, so to speak, unanchored and free-floating. Criteria of its allocation tend to be hotly contested, while the customary sequence of the principle of allocation and its application is in a great number of cases reversed. The principle tends to be retrospectively articulated in the aftermath of the allocating decision or deduced from the already accomplished state of affairs. Nation-states find themselves sharing the conflict-ridden and quarrelsome company of actual, aspiring or pretending, but always pugnaciously competitive sovereign subjects, with entities

successfully evading the application of the heretofore binding triune principle of allocation, and all too often explicitly ignoring or stealthily sapping and impairing its designated objects.[4]

This intriguing scenario is in complete agreement with the image of 'liquid modernity' that has made Bauman famous, but it is quite distant from the position adopted by the present writer, who, at the beginning of the new millennium and hence even before Bauman, had actually proposed the term 'interregnum' as a key to interpreting our present.

In my book *The Passage West*, right from its first Italian edition (2003), the reader will come across lines recalling 'the current *interregnum* between the old inter-state framework and a new framework that has yet to be defined'[5]; or 'this *time suspended* between the *no-longer* of the old inter-state order and the not-yet of a new supranational order'[6]; or passages which – as Bauman was later to do in his works – define the suspended time of the interregnum via the term interlude: 'In this passage, European legal space risks situating itself in a no-man's-land, in a sort of *interlude* or time suspended between a '"democracy of identity" and a "democracy of differences". Despite Habermas' hopes, we are still far from a theory and a praxis able to legitimize itself through the "inclusion of the Other"'.[7]

Carl Schmitt's Concept of the Political in Today's World Picture

Bauman appears to ignore, or to overlook, the retrieval of Carl Schmitt's concept of the Political and the redevelopments of the notion of the 'state of exception' that have marked philosophical debates in Italy since the 1970s.[8] At the same time, he provides an all-too-linear picture of the dynamics of globalization, without grasping the copresence (and at times conflictual coexistence) within them of opposite tendencies: deterritorialization and reterritorialization, diffusion and concentration, and interdependence and diaspora. This is why – like some of the authoritative authors featured in the present volume – I have stressed on the need for a more rigorous lexicon and conceptual 'toolbox', by suggesting we switch from deconstructive conformism to a reconstructive phase.

In a book published in 2008 I wrote:

If we truly wish to face the global risk lurking in the *current interregnum between the old Westphalian order and the new and still inceptive world order*, we must accomplish a drastic conversion from the deconstructive to the reconstructive phase. At a time in which deconstruction has become a kind of new conformism in all fields, it is necessary to reconstruct – which is to say, to conceptually redefine – the great plan of modern universalism, starting no longer from the *logic* of identity, but from the *criterion* of difference.[9]

Diaspora e interregno is the title of a section of the same book devoted to the fate of law in a 'post-Hobbesian order' (to use what has become a classic expression by Philippe Schmitter).[10]

The construction of a new concept of the Political capable of going beyond Carl Schmitt and Antonio Gramsci – the two theorists who, from opposite sides, had best grasped the change in form that politics was undergoing well into the twentieth century – must place three fundamental aspects at the centre of its analysis today.

First of all, the epistemological turn brought about by the emergence of political economy. Marx – the mature Marx of the *Grundrisse* and *Capital* – had perfectly grasped the sharply innovative character of that new science which combined into an oxymoron two terms that the Classical tradition had kept separate: the *oikos*, the domestic sphere of material production–reproduction; and the *polis*, the sphere of politics as the praxis of public governance. From Adam Smith onwards, the aim and source of the State's legitimacy was no longer the 'good life', but the 'wealth of the Nation'. Smith paid close attention to the interconnection between economics, politics, and law, aware of the fact that the market's 'invisible hand' needs the State's 'visible hand' in order to function.

Secondly, the coexistence of two principles in the five 'long centuries' of modernity: the principle of 'globality' and that of 'territoriality'. These themes occur in the works of Giovanni Arrighi, an economic sociologist with an eye for history,[11] and of Charles Maier, a historian who pays close attention to the political and social sciences.[12] The former has provided a crucial contribution to the analysis of the globalized world, not least from a comparative perspective. The latter has brought into focus the features of 'Leviathan 2.0', i.e. the form of State that established itself between the mid-nineteenth and mid-twentieth centuries, suggesting that one of the paradoxical effects of the digital age has been the decline of the paradigm of governance through the establishment of a 'Leviathan 3.0' and a return to the logic of territorial boundaries.

Thirdly, the non-interchangeability of the concepts of 'capital' and 'capitalism'. As I have already argued in my book *Dopo il Leviatano*,

> the dominance of global capital does not give rise to a single, standardized version of capitalism (a term which is actually foreign to the Marxian vocabulary and which only attained a scientific standing with Sombart and Weber), but rather to a multiplicity of 'capitalisms'.[13]

These 'capitalisms' – and we here get to the crucial point – differ not only from an ethnic–cultural perspective but also, especially, from a political standpoint.

Max Weber and the 'Political Capitalism'

In the age of global hyper-modernity, we thus witness the reproduction of the form of 'political capitalism', which Max Weber had envisaged in §31 of *Wirtschaft und Gesellschaft*, where he had presented it as an anomalous itera-tion, compared to the rationality of modern Western capitalism. This anomaly outlines a new global world that is far from 'liquid', a world dominated by an antagonistic duumvirate of political capitalisms – the United States and China – that encapsulate the economic, mercantile, and technological dynamic within a logic and strategy of power.[14]

This new bipolar version of what Weber calls *politischer Kapitalismus* would not appear to bode well for the future of the planet and its peoples. It is already creating a series of conflictual fault lines: from the fault line of inequality, which is now progressively impoverishing the middle classes in developed countries, to the identitarian conflicts between territorial nation-alities and trans-territorial diasporic communities. This perennial instability has given rise to a post-hegemonic configuration of the world, marked by a crisis of authority on a global scale. This crisis brings into play the prob-lem of a *horizontal reconstruction of the Political* hinging on the web of subjectivities and individual differences. The contributions featured in the present volume focus precisely on such topics: the relation (and possible transition) between biopolitics and post-hegemony, the genealogy of the subject, the redefinition of the concept of community, and the multitude-people hendiadys.

The populist syndrome is at once a symptom and a constitutive fac-tor of this crisis of authority. In its twofold form as political populism and digital-media-videocratic neopopulism, the populist phenomenon represents a problem that is wholly *internal* to the dynamics of the transformation of democracy.[15] This is a problem that can be traced back to the very origins of Western democracy: like all foundational terms, the word 'people' is sub-ject to that indeterminacy principle that makes it the underlying energy and legitimizing power of democracy. Yet the people is not merely a concept or a subject – both of which, by definition, are nowhere to be found. The people is also a people-event: a driving force of history.

This leads us to the threshold of the 'other stage' of our introductory chap-ter. And, as we shall see, on this new stage of the interregnum, the first pillar of the Political to be put under stress will be precisely the Weberian paradigm of the legitimation of power.

However, in writing about Weber now that more than a centenary has passed since his death, we should always remember – which is to say, always cherish in our hearts and minds – the closing words of the 'Politik als Beruf' lecture, with which this great theoretician of 'disenchantment', instead of reducing politics to the art of what is possible, placed it in direct relation to the *impossible*:

Politics is a strong and slow boring of hard boards. It takes both passion and perspective. Certainly all historical experience confirms the truth – that man would not have attained the possible unless time and again he had reached out for the impossible.[16]

Notes

1 A. Gramsci, *Quaderni del carcere*, Edizione critica dell'Istituto Gramsci, ed. by Valentino Gerratana, Vol. I, *Quaderni 1-5 (1929–1932)*, Einaudi, Torino 1975, Q 3 (XX), § 34 (*Passato e presente*), p. 311; here quoted after A. Gramsci, *Selections from the Prison Notebooks*, ed. and trans. Quentin Hoare and Geoffrey Nowell Smith, Lawrence & Wishart, London 1971, p. 276. [Original text: "L'aspetto della crisi moderna che viene lamentato come «ondata di materialismo» è collegato con ciò che si chiama «crisi di autorità». Se la classe dominante ha perduto il consenso, cioè non è più «dirigente», ma unicamente «dominante», detentrice della pura forza coercitiva, ciò appunto significa che le grandi masse si sono staccate dalle ideologie tradizionali, non credono più a ciò in cui prima credevano, ecc. La crisi consiste appunto nel fatto che il vecchio muore e il nuovo non può nascere: in questo interregno si verificano i fenomeni morbosi più svariati. A questo paragrafo devono essere collegate alcune osservazioni fatte sulla cosí detta «quistione dei giovani», determinata dalla «crisi di autorità» delle vecchie generazioni dirigenti e dal meccanico impedimento, posto a chi potrebbe dirigere, di svolgere la sua missione. Il problema è questo: una rottura cosí grave tra masse popolari e ideologie dominanti come quella che si è verificata nel dopoguerra, può essere «guarita» col puro esercizio della forza che impedisce a nuove ideologie di imporsi? L'interregno, la crisi di cui si impedisce cosí la soluzione storicamente normale, si risolverà necessariamente a favore di una restaurazione del vecchio? Dato il carattere delle ideologie, ciò è da escludere, ma non in senso assoluto."]
2 Z. Bauman, "Times of Interregnum", in *Ethics & Global Politics*, Vol. 5, No. 1, 2012, pp. 49–56. With regard to the political powerlessness of Europe, see also Étienne Balibar, 'Interregnum', in Id., *Europe, crise et fin?*, Le Bord de l'eau, Lormont 2016, pp. 7–31.
3 Z. Bauman, op. cit., pp. 49–50.
4 Ibid., p. 50.
5 G. Marramao, *The Passage West*, Verso, London-New York 2012, p. 132 (original ed., *Passaggio a Occidente*, Bollati Boringhieri, Torino 2003). In the United States, The University of Michigan Library has devoted a volume to this book: 'On Giacomo Marramao's "The Passage West"', *Política Común*, Special Issue, Vol. 8, Michigan Publishing, Ann Arbor 2015 (It. transl., *Filosofia dei mondi globali. Conversazioni con Giacomo Marramao*, ed. by Stefano Franchi and Manuela Marchesini, Bollati Boringhieri, Torino 2017 – contributions by Peter Baker, Martin Jay, Andy Lantz, Alberto Moreiras, Pedro Ángel Palou, Carlos Rodriguez, Teresa M. Vilarós, and Hayden White).
6 G. Marramao, *The Passage West*, cit., p. 41. The full sentence reads as follows: 'Due to the political void produced by the absence of global governance and of a legitimate institutional mediation (at this **time** suspended between the *no-longer* of the old inter-state order and the *not-yet* of a new supranational order), the *sides of universalism and of differences stand in opposition, exacerbating their respective one-sidedness and* hardening their position in the glocal pincer. The tension released from the *double bind* takes on the shape of a *conflict of identities* whose logic escapes the procedural *dispositifs* of control of contemporary "polyarchies"'.
7 Ibid., pp. 211–212.

8   In the academic year 1977–1978, I held a course on 'The Concept of the Political in Carl Schmitt' at the University of Naples "L'Orientale", where I was teaching at the time (this was the first course on Schmitt held in an Italian university after the Second World War). I also took Schmitt as a term of comparison for 'the Marxisms' of the interwar period in my book *Il Politico e le trasformazioni*, De Donato, Bari 1979 (now published in an updated English edition under the title *The Bewitched World of Capital: Economic Crisis and the Metamorphosis of the Political*, ed. by Matteo Mandarini, Brill, Leiden-Boston 2023).

9   G. Marramao, *La passione del presente*, Bollati Boringheri, Torino 2008, p. 42.

10   Cf. ibid., pp. 181 ff.

11   See G. Arrighi, *The Long Twentieth Century: Money, Power, and the Origins of Our Times*, new edition, Verso, London-New York 2009.

12   Ch. S. Maier, *Leviathan 2.0: Inventing Modern Statehood*, Harvard University Press, Cambridge, MA 2012; *Once Within Borders: Territories of Power, Wealth and Belonging since 1500*, Harvard University Press, Cambridge, MA 2016.

13   G. Marramao, *Dopo il Leviatano*, new ed., Bollati Boringhieri, Torino 2013, pp. 463–464.

14   On this topic, see the recent volume by A. Aresu, *Le potenze del capitalismo politico: Stati Uniti e Cina*, La Nave di Teseo, Milano 2020.

15   See P. Rosanvallon, "Penser le populisme", in *La vie des idées*, 27 September 2011. Even Umberto Coldagelli – a notable historian and intellectual belonging to the Italian 'workerist' tradition – has highlighted the 'populist' features of the presidentialism of the Fifth Republic: see U. Coldagelli, *La quinta repubblica da De Gaulle a Sarkozy*, Donzelli, Roma 2009.

16   M. Weber, "Politik als Beruf" (1918), in *Gesammelte politische Schriften*, Duncker & Humblot, Munich 1921, p. 450; English translation, "Politics as a Vocation", in M. Weber, *Essays in Sociology*, trans. and ed. by H.H. Gerth and C. Wright Mills, Oxford University Press, New York 1946, p. 128.

2 The Other Scene

On Populist Syndrome: Delegitimization as a Political Strategy

From Legitimate Power to Delegitimized Power

The tradition of social thought that, from Max Weber onwards, has established the problem of legitimation at the centre of the analysis of power is now facing serious difficulties, owing to the paradoxical transformation which has occurred in the logic of democratic systems. Political conflict appears to be increasingly polarized through the opposite tendency towards delegitimization. Parties, movements, and agencies competing for the acquisition of power seem to no longer be directing their action towards legitimizing their own ideas and programmes but rather towards the delegitimization of their opponents. A radical or even antagonistic kind of competition based on mutual recognition between competing factions has increasingly come to be replaced by the disavowal and disrepute of the opponent as a privileged means of acquiring the sort of 'political surplus value' capable of ensuring stable popular consensus.

The thesis I wish to submit is that the shifting of the centre of gravity in democratic competition from the problem of legitimization to the strategy of delegitimization represents the common denominator among the many variants of the phenomenon referred to by vague terms such as 'populism', 'national-populism', and 'sovereignism'. Following the transition from the democracy of parties to the 'democracy of the public'[1] – marked by the decline of the political cultures of the post–Second World War period, by the destructuring of mass parties, and by a twofold process of personalization and mediatization – the phenomenon in question has spelt the dawn of a new era for democratic dynamics. This era is characterized by what I would define as the 'populist syndrome', something which Ilvo Diamanti and Marc Lazar have instead described using the memorable term 'popolocrazia' ('people-cracy').[2] Through their delegitimizing aggressiveness and 'rejection of any sort of politics', populist movements today represent 'the manifestation of a democratic problem' while at the same time standing as the 'expression of and means towards what are perhaps crucial metamorphoses of our democracies'.[3]

But here the first problem emerges: to what extent does the common denominator of delegitimization mark a truly new phenomenon, as opposed to the re-emergence – in other forms and in a different historical context – of

DOI: 10.4324/9781032632827-2

what has been a constitutive factor of Western democracy from its very origins? Addressing a key issue such as that of delegitimization in an eminently comparative historical and linguistic – rather than merely political – context calls for a preliminary word of caution.

Clearly, this is a burning issue: the cross-sectional nature of 'delegitimizing rhetoric' in the various European political systems (and, to an almost grotesque level, in US democracy) is such a manifest phenomenon that one does not need particularly sophisticated analytical tools to detect it. However, it is only possible to grasp its actual impact by viewing the present from a distance through the use of what Carlo Ginzburg would call an 'inverted telescope'.

Only by adopting this reverse perspective is it possible to grasp that *untimely fold of the present* capable of bringing out enduring features and changes, forms of continuity and breaks, the past of what is new and the memory of the future. Delegitimization – a term coined in relatively recent times, but which has spread to almost all Western languages – designates a 'characteristic aspect of the contemporary political sphere' and a 'symbolic-discursive mode of political propaganda', as historian Fulvio Cammarano has shown. However, delegitimization practices have de facto been at work from the very start in this field, which in Classical Greece was defined – according to Christian Meier's famous reconstruction[4] – using a substantivized adjective that was destined to emerge as one of the central categories in our vocabulary: *politics*.

Delegitimization and State of Exception

Since, for obvious reasons, this is not the place where to newly present the kind of genealogical reconstructions I have offered elsewhere,[5] I will limit myself to a few observations. Their aim will be to highlight the logically asymmetrical and historically discontinuous relationship between the pairs of terms legitimacy/illegitimacy and legitimization/delegitimization: the former constituted by a vertical axiality of a structural-regulatory sort and the latter by a horizontal axiality of the historical-dynamic sort.

Very succinctly, the use of the non-*legitimus* argument as a strategic weapon to devalue political opponents marks the whole history of political theory and praxis in the West, starting from the development of the concept of the 'political' in Greece through the distinction between what is in compliance with the *koinonia*, the shared space of the *polis*, and what is not. The etymology of *legitimus*, like the Greek term *nomimon*, suggests a relationship based on compliance with the law. But the law in question here is originally *Nomos*: the supreme ordering principle – *Nomos basileus*, as illustrated by Marcello Gigante[6] and later, in the footsteps of Carl Schmitt, by Pier Paolo Portinaro[7] – that is irreducible to the positive law established by *kratos*, yet shaped and permeated by justice. Therefore, all real *nomimon* is also *dikaion*.

We thus witness the emergence of a recurrent ethical feature that – periodical turns and breaks notwithstanding – runs through all the various stages of ancient and medieval natural law, down to contractualism and modern constitutionalism. Here the fundamental principles of the Constitution receive a legitimizing/delegitimizing *potestas*, an inclusive/exclusive power, as a *trait d'union* between law and politics (or, better, between the regulatory axioms of law and the informative principles of politics).

However, in the natural law tradition itself, the question of legitimacy acquires a crucial role: in the form of a circle between the validity and the effectiveness of the legal system (Hans Kelsen), as the simultaneously effective and symbolic surplus value of charisma (Max Weber), or through a reference to the 'state of exception' as a 'force of law' that is extra-legal (yet not extra-juridical, i.e. which cannot be confused with mere force) and which at its core carries a legitimacy that exceeds legality (Carl Schmitt). Schmitt's famous formula 'Sovereign is he who decides the state of exception' would thus come to mean: 'Sovereign is he who decides on legitimacy', i.e. 'Sovereign is he who has the power to legitimately proclaim the suspension of the law'.

Hence the crucial question: On the basis of what criterion can we define the dimension and subject of legitimacy? Schmitt identifies this criterion in the constitutive antithesis of the Political: the dividing line between friend and enemy. Only he who is capable of tracing this line has the legitimacy to proclaim the state of exception. Yet this does not at all delegitimize one's enemy (understood as *hostis*, or public enemy, as opposed to *inimicus*, or private enemy): in fact, he receives full acknowledgement as a legitimate opponent. On the other hand, Weber identifies the common denominator of the three ideal forms of legitimate power (traditional, rational–legal, and charismatic) – which are only distinguishable on the epistemic level, whereas in practice they are intertwined – in the *belief* of 'the governed'. However, it must be noted that, from Weber's perspective, 'belief in legitimacy' constitutes not an *effect* but a *source* of power (hence the radical difference between his view and Foucault's, for instance).

From Pluralism to the Polytheism of Values

In accordance with the paradigmatic assumption of legal positivism, the surplus or tension between legitimacy and legality still falls within a vertical kind of axiality centred on the relation between those who govern and those who are governed. Not least for this reason, as the analysis formulated by Guglielmo Ferrero many years ago suggests,[8] the transition to democratic legitimacy is destined to prove difficult. However, despite the endurance of motifs that flow throughout the history of Western politics as an underground current, the issues at stake change considerably once we pass from the vertical axiality of legitimate–illegitimate to the horizontal one of legitimization–delegitimization as a *process*.

As Reinhart Koselleck has shown in his studies on the transformation of the socio-political lexicon in the modern age,[9] the turning point at which the new constellation of the dynamic terms of modernity emerged (from the neologism *Weltgeschichte*, 'Universal history' or 'World-history', to the semantic redefinition of terms such as rogress, revolution, and liberation) must be placed between the mid-eighteenth and the mid-nineteenth centuries. In this period of crucial transformations, we witness the emergence of new pairs of opposites (to mention only the most influential: revolution–reaction, progress–conservation, right–left, nationalism–cosmopolitanism) that fostered incompatible world views. Their tendency towards mutual delegitimization gives rise to a horizontal axiality, which is exactly the reverse of the horizontalness of the pact: the axiality of the conflict of values.

From being an assumption, legitimization is thus turned into an objective or thing at stake. It no longer coincides – as in Weber's famous threefold division of forms of legitimate power – with conformity to tradition (to the authority of the 'eternal yesterday'), commitment to the charismatic power of a leader or movement, or reliance on the 'power of the law', but rather with a rhetorical-strategic device for devaluation. Nevertheless, the scenario of a 'polytheism of values' now comes across as a genuine prophecy in the face of the conflicts over identity that are tearing Europe and the whole globalized world apart. This is only the case, however, if this scenario is not mistaken for an edifying praise of the pluralism and ethical relativism of points of view (*Standpunkte*) but is grasped in terms of a tragic exclusiveness of points of attack (*Angriffspunkte*) engaged in a fatal dispute. In this case too, however, it is a matter of distinguishing between a conflict of values which Schmitt himself regarded as worse and deadlier than Hobbes' *bellum omnium contra omnes* and the strategies of mutual delegitimization adopted by political rivals pursuing objectives pertaining to the seizing of power.

The People and Its Double

The delegitimization practices characterizing democratic societies fall along a shadow line, a boundary between law, politics, and morality: a hybrid symbolic space, steeped in ideological influences, summary narratives, and a rhetoric of discredit which, through the new media, use history as a means of self-legitimization, with selective or sometimes arbitrary flippancy. In the metamorphoses that have affected the public sphere, the legitimization/delegitimization antithesis thus implies a web-like system of references between discursive practices, strategic logics, and identitarian dynamics.

The effects of political communication are not merely cognitive, as they also affect the performative power of words across different pragmatic-linguistic contexts. The adoption of a perspective centred on the intertwining of historical semantics, linguistics, and cultural analysis not only makes it possible to bring into focus the systemic nature of contrastive identity – to consider the case of Italy – but opens up the path to a medium-/long-term reconstruction of the 'divisiveness' which marks the country's political history. The rift in question does not concern only its republican phase – through the well-known phenomenon of *conventio ad excludendum*, a legacy of the 'long civil war of the 20th century' – but can be traced back to the very origins of the process of Italian political unification.

Indeed, the theme of 'two nations' or 'two peoples' was put forward as early as 1868 by Angelo Camillo De Meis in his essay 'Il Sovrano', republished by Benedetto Croce in 1927, along with a polemic against Carducci and Fiorentino: 'As long as modern society is divided into two peoples' – De Meis wrote – 'a middle ground will always be necessary where they can meet and reach some mutual understanding [...]. In Italy the two modern Peoples are deeply separated; more than elsewhere, perhaps, because it is the centre and headquarters of the religion of Celtic-Latin Europe. They cannot understand each other, and they are naturally divided into two opposite and enemy camps. Therefore, no real and perfect Sovereignty is possible, but only Tyranny'.[10]

We shall soon turn to consider the significance of these observations for the issue of memory and its multidimensionality. First, though, there is a question we must address.

Community and the Citizenship Gap

Delegitimization is no doubt a recurrent feature of political conflict: we need to only consider Machiavelli's 'iniurie' ('injuries'). But precisely for this reason, just like conflict *sans phrase*, it risks proving an empty vessel. It can only produce effects in terms of knowledge if it is set in relation to specific contexts and contents. Today, political conflict appears to be permeated by ethical, religious, and anthropological elements: far from being accessory, the elements are constitutive of identitarian logics that have taken the place of the ideological frameworks known (and experienced) over the last two years of modernity. These have been long centuries: the twentieth century too was not a short one – indeed, Giovanni Arrighi has rightly referred to it as 'the long 20th century'.

At the turn of the twenty-first century, we have witnessed the failure of the two primary models of citizenship integration theorized and practised over the course of modernity: the universalist–assimilationist republican model and the strong differentialist–multiculturalist model – what Seyla Benhabib has described as the 'mosaic' model. It is an irony of history that the 'République model' and the 'Londonistan model' give rise to the same forms of identitarian conflict, marked by the transition from the logic of the rational assessment of one's interests to the logic of belonging (or of 'conversion', to borrow Alessandro Pizzorno's term).[11]

To complicate matters, the globalized world finds itself in a sort of 'interregnum' between the 'no longer' of the old order based on sovereign nation states and the 'not yet' of a post-national order which, after having struggled to take shape, now appears to be caving in upon itself, by raising anachronistic borders and coagulating into a geopolitics and geoeconomics of large spaces dominated by continent-states: from the United States to China and from India to Russia and Brazil. In this interregnum, as in all interregnums, monstrous hybrids are already coming to light that might spell the end of that complex of knowledge and practices which for the past 2,500 years we have called Politics.

One of these hybrids is that mix of 'anti-politics' (a misleading polemical term used to describe anti-establishment movements) and hyper-democratic rhetoric that characterizes the double nature of the People in populist movements. The People presents itself, on the one hand, as a homogeneous and identity-shaping entity and, on the other, as 'the virtuous people against its corrupt representatives', whose sovereignty can only be reaffirmed by a leader capable of embodying its will.[12]

However, there is also a theoretically more sophisticated version of populism which is largely overlooked by mainstream political science. It stands in open contrast to the 'anti-political' and delegitimizing tendency and hedges its bets on the 'populist moment' as the only possible means of ensuring the 'return of the Political' from the perspective of a radical democracy, yet not an 'immediate democracy'[13] – an antagonistic, yet at the same time, pluralistic and anti-authoritarian democracy. Without engaging with this theoretically strong proposal, any attempt to make sense of the populist syndrome is bound to be purely illusionary.

Political Populism

When I speak of the theoretically strong proposal of *political populism*, what I am referring to, in particular, is the work carried out by Ernesto Laclau in the philosophical field and by Chantal Mouffe in that of political science. To speak of the personality, philosophical work, passion, and political commitment of Ernesto Laclau, today is difficult for anyone, given the complexity and relevance of his work.[14] But it is a particularly painful task for someone like the present writer, who was a friend of Laclau's and engaged with him, at different stages, across the two shores of the Atlantic from the late 1970s onwards. I can never forget our last meeting in Paris in December 2013, when the two of us served on the search committee for a post at the Sorbonne, together with Myriam Revault d'Allonnes, Pierre Rosanvallon, and other colleagues. Nor can I forget the lengthy email he sent me the day before his unexpected death in Seville on April 13, 2014, when he was taking part in a conference I too had meant to attend – having been forced to change my plans at the last minute. His remarkable contribution to the philosophical and political understanding of our times has been a focus of international debate for decades, following the publication of his famous 1985 book *Hegemony and Socialist Strategy*, co-authored by Chantal Mouffe; the 1996 essay *Emancipation(s)*; and the 2000 volume *Contingency, Hegemony, Universality* (written in collaboration with Judith Butler and Slavoj Žižek). It has acquired particular relevance with his 2005 book *On Populist Reason*. (In this context, however, we should not overlook Chantal Mouffe's contribution to the recovery, extension, and redefinition of Carl Schmitt's 'concept of the Political' in recent years: from the 2005 essay 'On the Political' to the 2018 volume *For a Left Populism*).

At a lecture given in Rome not long before his death, Laclau offered – in the clear and succinct form typical of oral presentations – a sort of 'secular arm' or *in actu* political translation of his main theoretical statements.[15] These statements revolve around the key notions of conflict, populism, and hegemony, and their radical redefinition from a discursive and – crucially, for this is where the theoretical core of his proposal lies – *anti-essentialistic* perspective. Without clearly grasping this assumption, namely Laclau's radical criticism of all forms of metaphysical substantialism or essentialism, it is impossible to understand the strictly *political* characterization of his notion of populism: a notion that conflicts with anti-political versions of populism that postulate the subject-people as an entity, which is already a given, already constituted.

On various occasions, Laclau had stressed how the 'social' presents itself with a marked degree of complexity and heterogeneity in contemporary societies. This does not imply the disappearance of the conflict between capital and labour that lies at the centre of the classic Marxian analysis of the capitalist mode of production. However, it requires its redefinition and re-contextualization in relation to the 'emergence of equally radical conflicts, such as the environmental, over common resources such as water, and frequent revolts against exclusion and social marginalization on a planetary scale'. The problem that emerges, then, is 'the political articulation of these conflicts': to think of politics is to think of a 'hegemonic practice' capable of recomposing into a unitary strategy a range of differences, conflicting polarities, and variety of demands that would otherwise be dispersed.

This theoretical plan for a recovery and overall reformulation of the Gramscian concept of hegemony – carried forth by Laclau through his close intellectual partnership with Chantal Mouffe, whose reflections on the 'Political', as already stressed, represent an original contribution and crucial complement to Laclau's own work – was presented as 'post-Marxist' from as early as 1985: with the publication, before the fall of the Berlin Wall, of their work *Hegemony and Socialist Strategy*. In this important book (which had a considerable influence on the international debate in the field), the theory of hegemony which Gramsci developed in his *Prison Notebooks* is, on the one hand, envisaged as the turning point for a break with Marx's 'economicism' and for a profound reassessment of the Leninist conception of politics. On the other hand, it is taken as a point of departure to be reformulated in terms of 'discourse theory'.

The reformulation of the concept of hegemony suggested by Laclau (and Mouffe) is achieved through a skilful combinatory logic, capable of combining and crossing – not without certain unresolved issues and internal tensions – five different theoretical coordinates: Saussure's linguistics, Lacanian psychoanalysis, the Gramscian legacy filtered through Althusser's *coupure épistémologique*, post-structuralism (in Derrida's, rather than Foucault's, version), and the cultural turn (adopted, with substantial changes, in Stuart Hall's version, starting from the second stage of British Cultural Studies and Postcolonial Studies). The outcome of this *ars combinatoria* is the tracing of the classic hendiadys economy/society, community/culture, and politics/hegemony back to discourse theory.

Anti-essentialism: The People as a Political Construction

'Discourse' is, therefore, the keyword in Laclau's theoretical programme: an *anti-essentialistic* assumption that dissolves all pre-established centrality, establishing political subjectivity within a hegemonic game based on a logic of inclusion/exclusion, openness/closure. The departure from the foundationalist perspective (even in its Marxist variants) has one crucial consequence, which is often overlooked by critics operating within mainstream political science. The Subject neither precedes nor establishes the discourse but, on the contrary, is the product of a 'subjectivization' process brought about by the discourse itself: more precisely – and more in keeping with Laclau's language – by discursive practices. In other words, originally there is no Subject, but only a Relation, understood not as 'the name of a *given* relational concept',[16] but as a constellation of actions and relational practices that always make the subjects. Within this constellation – the primary setting for society – there are no substantial identities (be they of an individualistic or community sort) but only conflicting polycentric dynamics between irreducible *differences*. Hence the reason why, again in keeping with the anti-essentialistic assumption, just as there are no pre-established individual subjects (as conceived in modern contractualism, from Hobbes onwards), according to Laclau there cannot be any 'society' as a presupposed totality or spontaneous pullulation (in Durkheim's sense or in that of the various forms of holism, from Aristotle to contemporary communitarians).

For Laclau, as much as for Cornelius Castoriadis, [17]society does not exist except as an 'imaginary institution'. What sociologists and cultural anthropologists call the 'social bond' is actually the contingent result of discursive practices whose logic always coincides with a strategy aimed at domination. The notion of 'discourse', then, far from ultimately amounting to a linguistic-communicative modality, indicates the construction of a relational context of meaning whose shifting epicentre – what is at stake – is represented by the question of power.

Here we find another crucial step in Laclau's theory: just as, based on such promises, it has become meaningless to distinguish between logic and strategy (since power is not a superstructure but a constitutive factor within language itself), so the Foucaultian distinction between discursive and non-discursive practices, 'words' and 'things', language and praxis, loses all meaning.

Right from its grammatical and syntactical structure, the order of the discourse presents itself as an *inextricable web between material dimension and symbolic sphere*. From this perspective, not only the social structure but the 'economy' itself, released from its fetishized objectivity, presents itself as a complex articulation of relational and practical-discursive differences. In one respect, this aspect was already foreshadowed by Marx through the notion of 'relations of production'; in another respect, it has become crystallized into what is still a classic treatment, revolving around the distinction between basic structure and superstructure. Discourse theory, which is played out in the pair of terms signifier/signified, resolves the aporia inherent in the Marxian topic, insofar as the symbolic dimension of 'meaning' and 'culture' is removed from the superstructural level and grafted upon the fabric of the constitutive practices of 'material' relations themselves.

But – and the weight of this *but* cannot be overstated, for without it we would risk trivializing Laclau's position almost to the point of making a caricature of it – there is no discursive context capable of standing as a saturated totality in which the 'sign' is realized in the 'meaning', in which signifiers resolve all possible meanings within themselves. Herein lies the crucial function exercised within Laclau's reflection by a particularly sophisticated and conceptually challenging leitmotiv, which I can only briefly outline here: the theme of the 'empty signifier'. The constitutively partial character of an 'order of discourse' whose logic is always strategically oriented imposes the ineluctable destiny of partiality and contingency on that order.

Only in the light of these premises is it possible to understand what might at first sight seem like a provocative statement by Laclau, who affirms the perfect coincidence between populism and politics (this statement already occurs in the final chapter of his first work, *Politics and Ideology in Marxist Theory: Capitalism, Fascism, Populism*, published in 1977, and it is further developed in the first chapter of *Hegemony and Socialist Strategy*). Just like discourse, the signifier People presents itself as something akin to what mathematicians call an 'unsaturated formula': a signifier liable to acquire different meanings, depending on the context, but never to realize all its possible meanings in itself. However, the emptier this signifier is, the more it must logically and strategically present itself as a totality. For this simple yet decisive reason, the hidden meaning of the People as a political construct must always be discovered in its implicit – i.e. (in Freudian terms of *Verdrängung* and *Verwerfung*) repressed, yet precisely for this reason constitutive – reference to a 'reject', an excluded remainder: women, slaves, and foreigners with respect to the Greek *demos*, the *plebs* with respect to the Roman *populus*. Besides, gazing back at the oldest democracy of modernity, who could ever deny the non-descriptive but performative character of the formula, '*We, the People*'?

Moving on from theoretical statements to more strictly political ones, Laclau's aim is to bind together populism and radical democracy, based on a hegemonic strategy designed to cross the boundary that separates the people from its remainder, by translating the logic of difference (the sum of dispersed demands addressed to power) into an 'equivalencial logic' that aligns these claims around an 'empty signifier'. Laclau is lucidly aware that even the most democratically inclusive operation will nonetheless produce a remainder: a marker of the contingency of all hegemonic practices and, at the same time, a guarantee of the opening up of conflicts and dynamics of change. A work of translation of this sort can never lead to the solving or neutralizing of conflict; rather, it always implies the construction of an antagonistic boundary between the 'people' and the authorities.

'Radical politics for me means the political construction of the people', Laclau repeatedly stated. Yet the political construction of the people occurs inside and outside the State simultaneously: inside the State, as the conflict over the acknowledgement of particular interests; outside the State, as it 'challenges the monopoly of political decision-making'. For this reason, *populist politics should not be mistaken for a form of 'plebiscitarianism'*; on the contrary, it postulates a dynamic intertwining between direct and representative democracy. And it is precisely this intertwining that Laclau describes through the challenging expression 'radical democracy'.

A few more words to wrap up this whole issue. It has often been stressed that the populistic idea of Nation carries considerable risks in terms of abuse of power, intolerance, and the curtailment of liberty. Such concerns are far from ill-founded. However, Laclau has often responded by stressing how, in Western democratic systems, the rhetoric centred on 'empty signifiers' such as Freedom, Civilization, and Justice in turn corresponds to a political-discursive strategy which, while on the surface asserting universality, actually engenders specific forms of discrimination and marginalization. The real risk in Laclau's theory of populism – a risk which critics have often overlooked – is instead of a radically opposite nature: it concerns the fragility of the project of the recomposition of differences that, within the new global constellation (however, we wish to interpret or represent it), hardly seem to fit with an idea of people and politics confined to the national paradigm.

I shall leave aside here the reservations of those people who, like the present writer, do not identify with 'populist reason', yet feel the need to stress the *cognitive dissonance* engendered by the divergent use of the term 'populism', or even 'homeland', in Europe and Latin America by distinguishing between Latin-American political populism and the xenophobic, media-driven neo-populism of Europe. However, we still need to consider the theoretical complexity and seriousness of the problem raised by Ernesto Laclau.

The anti-essentialistic perspective of his theoretical programme readily embraces the *pars destruens* of that great tradition in European thought which, from Hobbes to Kelsen (but also from Weber to Luhmann and Habermas himself), denies the People any real existence, taking instead a multitude of singularities and differences as its starting point. But whereas, in their *pars construens*, both Hobbes and Kelsen infer from this premise that the people is a juridical construct produced by the neutral device of sovereignty and/or that of the positive system of laws, the People represents a *political construct*: a construct without which the life and efficacy of the juridical order would lose all meaning. How can we deny, then, the untimely timeliness of this message? Still...

Power without Authority: The Double Regime of Memory

Still, a lot remains to be discussed, revised, and challenged.

First of all, there is the question of the double soul of modern democracy:

(a) the 'Madisonian' soul, with its principle of the limitation of power, including the power of the 'sovereign people'[18];
(b) the 'populist' soul, with the principle of participation.

This constitutive duplicity gives rise to the 'perennial tension within Western constitutionalism between *juridical limitation* and *political responsibility*' and, with it, the risk of two involutional tendencies: democracy without rights and rights without democracy.[19]

Second, there is the radical difference between Laclau and Mouffe's passionately political and engaging populism and the *media-driven neo-populism* of our digitalized societies. In the latter case, we find not a construction of the idea of a people, but its deconstruction and de-structuring into a mass of isolated individuals reduced to a mere audience, despite the illusion that it is possible for them to acquire a leading role through the Web. It is like a neo-Baroque spectatorial syndrome: *Spectator sum in hac scena, non actor....*

Therefore, in the so-called 'digital populism' of today – with its strategies of discredit and casual use of fake news, and 'formatted' states of exception, artfully constructed according to an 'occasionalism' that is light-years away from the great, tragic politics of the twentieth century – it is easy to see the other side of the neo-liberal breakdown of community bonds.

What destiny, then, awaits democratic polyarchies? There is only one way to attempt to regenerate democracy: by moving away from the language of legitimation/delegitimization for good, in order to recover the theme of authority.

This recovery, however, must coincide with a radical redefinition of the concept.[20] In the current interregnum, marked by *power without authority* and by *authority devoid of power*, it is necessary to sever the bond which keeps the idea of authority anchored in the *arché*, in the Principate–Principle, and to envisage it instead as an *auctoritas* understood – according to its etymology – as an *augere*, an *augmentum*, a symbolic growth and energy autonomously stemming from the dynamics of cooperation and conflict within the body politic. In other words, it is a matter of rethinking the Machiavellian motif of a generative, free, and cohesive republic, capable of forming a horizon of meaning for individual and collective action.

However, by now shifting our focus to the nexus between philosophy, politics, and history, we must envisage a process of constituting subjectivities capable – in the wake of the significant distinction introduced by Aleida Assmann[21] – of linking two different dimensions of memory:

(a) *function-memory*, in its twofold character: *selective*, insofar as it transmits foundational identity values, and *constructive* of a horizon of meaning for the community;
(b) *storage-memory*, which preserves the non-functional, the excluded, the 'surpassed', and – with it – 'the repository of lost opportunities', the alternatives excluded and defeated by individual and collective history, or unrealized, 'submerged', and latent possibilities.

Within the context of this layered vision of historical time, there is also an urgent need to rethink the time of politics and of its fields of action, beyond the classic antithesis between line and circle, cyclical and linear time.

By setting out from this, a counter-strategy must be developed capable of slowing down and inverting a deviation of democracy, which today appears to be increasingly marked by the populist syndrome.

Populism vs. People

In a passage from the 'American Lessons', Italo Calvino has a prophetic intuition about the threat hanging over our present. An existential epidemic, 'a pestilence has struck the human race in its most distinctive faculty – that is the use of words'.[22] A real 'language plague' that empties expressions of all density and 'cognitive force', dissolving them in the anonymity of abstract and multipurpose formulas in which every spark that springs from the clash of words with new circumstances is extinguished.

The laser gaze towards the future of this text from several decades ago is extraordinary, included in the cycle of Lectures that Calvino should have given at Harvard University and had signed before his death with the title *Six Memos for the Next Millennium*.

And it is inevitable that it refers us, in the current situation, to the fluid and generic way in which terms such as 'people' and 'populism' are treated today. Calvino knew, like few others, that the linguistic institution is the primary institution and that our speech acts inexorably determine the variables of exclusion and inclusion.

Following his idea of 'exactness' then leads us to highlight a peculiar phenomenon and a stake in the European political debate: people and populism are contrasting terms. Or, to take up the linguistic expressionism of Pierre Rosanvallon, they are two words that 'glare at each other'.[23]

Thus we have the paradox of making negative a term derived from the word that has always been at the basis of the idea of democracy. But to understand how things stand, we need to take a step forward, to see the root of the 'populist syndrome' precisely in a peculiar way of understanding the concept of the people.

'People' is one of those variable geometry concepts that in the West have always been constitutive of politics and its dilemmas: from the Greek *demos* to the Roman *civitas* to the medieval and modern idea of *people-nation*. If the people are the foundation of legitimacy and the driving force of the democratic system, their power remains undetermined. We can speak only in the abstract of the people understood in a juridical-normative sense, since we are dealing with a multitude of differences of gender, ethnicity, religion, and social condition (with the relative discriminations and hierarchy).

The people as a 'We', as an effective unity, can only be two things: a performative and inaugural statement, like the 'We, the People' that we find in the preamble of the Constitution of the United States, with its double soul 'Madisonian' (constitutional limitation of the majority principle) and 'populist' (promise to broaden participation); or a concrete historical subject, a *people-event* understood as an actor who intervenes in the political dynamics by directing or modifying its course even with revolutionary ruptures aimed at expanding the spaces of inclusion of democracy.

The people of European populist ideologies, on the other hand, escape both these perspectives, placing themselves in a no-man's land between the legal-formal indeterminacy and the plebiscitary indeterminacy that characterizes the various forms of totalitarianism. Even when it is presented in a more sophisticated form, meaning the people not as a pre-established substantial entity but as the result of a political construction, the neo-populist perspective does not escape two binding clauses common to all variants of populism: the assignment of the political construction of the People to a Leader (with the passage from 'We, the People' to 'I, the People') and the national-sovereign referent (with open hostility to 'stateless people' and to any form of cosmopolitanism).[24]

But in the meantime the modern trinomial, State–people–territory, has been upset by a global scene in which sovereignty has become 'sovereigntism', the people populism, and the territory is now being bypassed by the Net. With the inevitable, rapid obsolescence of self-styled charismatic leaders, determined by the unpredictability of the behaviour of the populations, less inclined to entrust themselves – as happened in the tragic century we have behind us – to a Chief who, as Theodor Adorno said, presents misfortune under the guise of salvation.

But in the meantime, very different trends are emerging outside the West on the world map, with power politics no longer of nation-states but of continent-states such as China, Russia, and India. This is the real, new challenge that awaits us.

Notes

1 As is widely known, the expression was first formulated by Bernard Manin, *Principes du gouvernement représentatif*, Calmann-Lévy, Paris 1995.
2 I. Diamanti-M. Lazar, *Popolocrazia. La metamorfosi delle nostre democrazie*, Laterza, Roma-Bari 2018.
3 Ibid., p. 7.
4 *Die Entstehung des Politischen bei den Griechen*, Suhrkamp, Frankfurt am Main 1980.
5 I am referring, in particular, to *The Passage West: Philosophy After the Age of the Nation State*, Verso, London-New York 2012.
6 See M. Gigante, *Nomos Basileus*, Edizioni Glaux, Napoli 1956 (new ed., Bibliopolis, Napoli 1993).
7 See P.P. Portinaro, *Appropriazione, distribuzione, produzione. Materiali per una teoria del "nomos"*, Angeli, Milano 1983; Id., *Il realismo politico*, Laterza, Roma-Bari 1999.
8 See G. Ferrero, *Potere. I geni invisibili della Città*, SugarCo, Milano 1981.
9 See R. Koselleck, *Zeitschichten. Studien zur Historik*, Suhrkamp, Frankfurt am Main 2000. I have engaged in an extended intellectual dialogue with Koselleck, as witnessed by my books *Potere e secolarizzazione* (1983), new and expanded ed., Bollati Boringhieri, Torino 2005; *La passione del presente. Breve lessico della modernità-mondo*, Bollati Boringhieri, Torino 2008; and *Dopo il Leviatano. Individuo e comunità* (1990), third, expanded ed., Bollati Boringhieri, Torino 2013 and 2017.
10 A.C. De Meis, *Il Sovrano. Saggio di Filosofia politica con riferenza all'Italia*, ed. by Benedetto Croce, Laterza, Bari 1927, pp. 13–14.
11 See the crucial collection of essays *Il velo della diversità. Studi su razionalità e riconoscimento*, Feltrinelli, Milano 2007.
12 See I. Diamanti-M. Lazar, *Popolocrazia*, cit., p. 8.
13 Condorcet uses this expression in the pamphlet *Aux amis de la liberté sur les moyens d'en assurer la durée* (1790), in *Œuvres de Condorcet*, t. X, Paris 1847, pp. 178–179.
14 I here draw upon some of the ideas I developed in the essay *Conflicto, populismo, hegemonía*, in "Debates y Combates", a. 5 (2015), Edición Homenaje. Ernesto Laclau, Vol. 2, pp. 63–70.
15 See E. Laclau, "Conflitto, populismo, egemonia", foreword by Giacomo Marramao, in *Parolechiave*, no. 52, 2014, pp. 67–74.
16 E. Laclau-C. Mouffe, *Hegemony and Socialist Strategy: Towards a Radical Democratic Politics*, Verso, London 1985, p. 93.
17 See C. Castoriadis, *L'institution inaginaire de la société*, Éditions du Seuil, Paris 1975.
18 James Madison, one of the founding fathers of American democracy, can rightly be considered a theorist of 'intermediate' democracy. He writes clearly as early as

the end of the eighteenth century that the representative republic will be superior to the direct democracies of the past because it will expose citizens less to two degenerations found in ancient democracies: anarchy, on the one hand, and, on the other hand, the interference of the majority on the freedom of individual citizens. To avoid these risks, modern democracy must apply two remedies: first, a federal structure, a form of state capable of reconciling democratic demands at the local level with the need for decisions on security and currency at the central level; second, the mediating function of representation.

19 See F. Raniolo, "Democrazie sotto stress e tendenze illiberali", in *Paradoxa*, a. XIII, No. 3, July–September 2019, p. 52.

20 For a recovery and redefinition of the theme of authority, in opposition to the logic of power, I will refer to the remarks I have put forward in *Against Power: For an Overhaul of Critical Theory*, Rowman and Littlefield, Lanham, MD 2016, following a theoretical path that is in many respects close to the "philosophy of difference": see esp. Luisa Muraro, *Autorità*, Rosenberg & Sellier, Torino 2013.

21 See A. Assmann, *Ricordare. Forme e mutamenti della memoria culturale*, Il Mulino, Bologna 2002.

22 I. Calvino, *Lezioni americane. Sei proposte per il prossimo millennio*, Garzanti, Milano 1988, p. 58; English translation, *Six Memos for the Next Millennium*, Harvard University Press, Cambridge, MA 1988, p. 56.

23 Among Pierre Rosanvallon's various cotributions on the issue of populism, see in particular *Le siècle du populisme: histoire, théorie, critique*, Seuil, Paris 2020.

24 It should be mentioned here that, in an essay a few years ago, Chantal Mouffe stigmatized the particular way in which 'right-wing populism' constructs its idea of the people. What characterizes 'right-wing' populist discourse is its strongly xenophobic character: immigrants are presented as a threat to the 'People's Identity' and any 'inclusive' vision of democracy is perceived as an imposition by elites against the real 'popular will'. See in this regard Chantal Mouffe, *La 'fin du politique' et le défi du populisme de droite*, first published in "Revue du M.A.U.S.S.", 2 (2002), pp. 178–194. The essay was later published in English translation under the title *The 'End of Politics' and the Challenge of Right-wing Populism*, in the volume *Populism and the Mirror of Democracy*, ed. by F. Panizza, Verso, London-New York 2005, pp. 50–71.

3   State of Exception

From Political Theology to History: Walter Benjamin's Messianism Without Waiting

The Messianic Cipher of Historical Materialism

No author has succeeded better than Benjamin in expressing the secret messianic figure that runs through, like a radical fissure, Marx's theory and, with it, the antagonistic structure of our present. It is this decisive circumstance that makes his famous theses 'on the concept of history' literally *extreme*: both testamentary and testimonial. A text addressed directly not only to all of us, understood collectively, but also to each and every one of us, to anyone capable of grasping its extraordinary internal tension and transposing its message: the clear shift of the concept of 'state of exception' from juridical and theological–political space, in which it had been elaborated by Carl Schmitt, to the dimension of historical time.

The interpretive key to Walter Benjamin's 'Theses on the Concept of History', which I intend to bring to light, can be deliberately and provocatively expressed in the title: 'Messianism without waiting'. This is literally a *para-doxical* title which seemingly contrasts with common sense or current opinion with regard to those characteristics traditionally attributed to the 'messianic'. How is it possible, in a literal sense, to have a messianism without 'horizon of delay?' And does not the lack of a 'wait' constitute sufficient reason for dissolving the very tension implied in the concept of a 'Messiah' itself? It is my firm conviction that one finds hidden here the secret cipher of a text – at once translucent and enigmatic – which can only be thoroughly grasped by reconstructing the multi-polar constellations of its conceptual and symbolic referents. That is, one cannot interpret its radical political–theological core simply as a 'secularized' version of messianism (as occurs in the philosophies of history criticized by Karl Löwith[1]): Benjamin's brand of messianism is in equal measure post-secular and post-religious. In short, the paradox of Benjamin's message of redemption lies in its position on the other side of the ambiguous Janus profile of Western Futurism. It is symbolized, on the one hand, by the promise of salvation in monotheistic religions and, on the other, by the modern philosophy of history's faith in progress. Hence, I will try to illustrate how the singular figure of a 'messianism without waiting' is tied to the proposal of a 'concept of history' not after the end of history, but rather, after the end of the *faith* in history.

DOI: 10.4324/9781032632827-3

Unsaturated Formulas

I will begin with a passage from the last letter from Benjamin to Adorno: a precious and intense document from a dialogue that became – despite well-known disagreements – increasingly close (the more intimate '*mein lieber Teddie*' instead of the formal '*Lieber Herr Wiesengrund*' with which their correspondence began on July 2, 1928, is telling in this regard). In this letter dated August 2, 1940 – sent (an irony of fate) from Lourdes – Benjamin seems to apply the political–theological constellation of the '*Grenzfall*' at the extreme hour of his own existence, the *extremus necessitatis casus*: 'Total uncertainty about what the next day, the next hour will bring has ruled my existence for many weeks'.[2] We have here, together, an absolute temporal contraction and a diametrical overturning of the messianic wait into a 'state of exception' (*Ausnahmezustand*): in the *Ernstfall* time carries a bipolar structure in which the extremes of Fear (*Angst*) and of Hope (*Hoffnung*) are hazardously related. This is a motif that appears throughout the radical thought of the twentieth century and which is echoed in Hölderlin's knotty adage: 'Where danger is there is salvation also'.

On the other hand, a recurring theme within the field of Benjaminian criticism argues that Benjamin developed his idea of messianism from reading the Romantics (in particular from *Christenheit oder Europa* by Novalis). This thesis is not completely correct and, on this point, Hermann Cohen provides an invaluable reference for reconstructing the sources and *Urszenen* (the symbolically prototypical scenes) of Benjamin's intellectual formation. Cohen's notion that history, properly defined, is a creation of the prophetic is of particular interest. Benjamin certainly draws from Novalis the idea of a 'plural' messiah ('with a million eyes'), but at the same time, he recognizes a tension between the neo-Kantian *Unendliche Aufgabe* and the Romantic idea of an infinite qualitative process. He halts in front of this tension and in a certain sense takes a step back, moving backwards in the direction of Leibniz's monad and thereby raising the question of unification and immanent unity. Above all, he poses the question of an Origin that is constantly unfulfilled and unrealizable (*unerfüllt* and *unerfüllbar*). This question paves the way for a perspective that can relate, in a manner that is as secret as it is resolute, the Benjaminian concept of history with cabbalistic tradition (especially with the cabbala of Yitzchak Luria, principal exponent in the sixteenth century of the Safed Cabbalistic school in Galilee). After all, it is not difficult to retrace in the enigmatic phrasing of thesis IX – 'make whole what has been smashed' (*das Zerschlagene zusammenfügen*)[3] – a messianic echo from Lurian doctrine of 'breaking vases'. A doctrine hinging on the concept of the *Zimzûm* (the idea of creation as an effect of the original withdrawal of God to leave space for the cosmos), of the *shevirath ha-kel'im* (the breaking of vases), which is at the origins of evil, and of the *tiqqu'n* understood as the necessary and consequent restoration of broken unity. And yet ...

And yet the Benjaminian messiah and the cabbala intersect at a specific point: the fulfillment of creation is the task of human action. Thus, if we read Benjamin's theses against Heidegger's last appeal we are struck by a paradoxical inversion: while for Heidegger 'only a God can save us', for Benjamin *only man can save God*. A paradox which is intimately Jewish and which sheds light on the meaning that the category of redemption comes to assume within the constellation of 'postponements' outlined in the numerous drafts of that radical and extreme text: *Über den Begriff der Geschichte*.

Another theme, which incidentally appears in re-reading some current commentaries of Benjamin, consists of the remembrance/reawakening nexus, a nexus some have seen as evidence of neo-Platonic traces in Benjamin. Despite my own doubts as to the value of this hypothesis as an interpretive key, I find it nonetheless useful and productive: it allows us to think of Benjamin not just from a theological perspective but also *in the strictest sense* from a philosophical one (this seems to me important in light of the old and new prejudices of academic philosophy with regard to Benjamin's work).

Representation and Concept

We must therefore return to the thesis to re-focus the argument. The first aspect of our re-reading speaks to theme. Here what is decisive is the programmatic character of the title. Benjamin, as I have already noted, speaks of the concept (*Begriff*) of history: that is, a history that, while reduced to a concept, remains as a central (and still problematic) referent of discourse. We are not speaking, therefore, of theses *on the end* of history but rather of theses *on history* as they are thought and expressed in the 'end-time'. I will argue that the messianic, instead of capping the 'end of time', coincides with humanity's return to its *simply historical* role. That is, it coincides with the representation (*Darstellung*) of a humanity that is finally liberated from the naturalized history of Progress (*Fortschritt*) and Domination (*Herrschaft*). Our hermeneutic task consists in escaping the pitfall of misunderstanding produced by tendentious and prejudicial critiques, including the polemical remarks of Adorno himself who, in his *Negative Dialectics*, seems to chide Benjamin (whom he recognizes as having taught him the necessity of crossing the 'iron desert of abstraction' (*Eisenwüste der Abstraktion*) to arrive rigorously at concrete philosophizing) on his inability to explode the philosophical devices of *Begriffslogik* (the logic of the concept). In truth, Benjamin's insistence on the concept must be viewed in direct relation to the decline of a messianic motif in the 'mode of exposition' (*Darstellungsweise*) of Marxist dialectics. For this reason, the theses should not be read as an omni-comprehensive key – as a sort of philosophico-historical summa – but as an incandescent laboratory of experimental concepts and thoughts. They are marked by a clear syncretism, in which the boundaries between what are extremely diverse symbolic registers (those of messianism, eschatology, and the apocalypse, represented by the figure of the Antichrist) disappear. It is through this 'syncope' of heterogeneous elements that the theses continue to exercise an extraordinary power of suggestion: they give form to a *withheld pathos*. Up until the very end, Benjamin tried to polish the text, carefully distilling the words, choosing with singular exactness the nouns and adjectives, directing his argument towards a precise conclusion: to perform a symbolic conversion (and not a generically metaphorical or analogical one) between the twin axes of messianism and historical materialism. But – this is the crucial point – the figure of the conversion is provided by a specific criterion that has been transformed from the area of political theology. Without the political theology of the *Ausnahmezustand* – and here an obligatory reference is due to the work of Jacques Derrida and Giorgio Agamben – the possibility of reciprocal convergence and conversion between these two axes would remain a moot point.

At this point we cannot but advance serious doubts on Jacob Taubes' reading of Benjamin's political theology. In particular, I am referring to his thesis of a Gnostic Benjamin, a modern Marcionite (*moderner Marcionit*), founded on Benjamin's anti-immanentism and presented as the criterion of the real and true inversion of the Spinoza–Nietzschean line.[4] This thesis, it seems to me, is both controversial and problematic. Taubes focuses on a decisive issue: Benjamin read Nietzsche with extreme interest, while his most acute and bitter hostilities were directed at Heidegger (a fact that is difficult to evade or overlook). Taubes certainly provides an illuminating contribution by proposing a tripartite comparison of Benjamin, Schmitt, and Karl Barth (recently revisited by Agamben and Badiou), which he situates against the backdrop of Paul's messianism. Taubes, however, misses the mark in considering the themes discussed in Benjamin's work as incompatible with the theme of secularization. This critique is rightly underscored by Michele Ranchetti in his introduction to the Italian edition of *Abendländische Eschatologie*: in any case, the question of secularization makes little sense from Taubes' viewpoint since he assumes that secularization, as a purely historiographical question, is incapable of capturing the persistence of the sacred and its reappearance in the modern era.[5]

I contend, on the other hand, that for Benjamin secularization is tied to the theme of the persistence of the sacred (and not to its dissolution), but in a specifically polemical sense. The theme of secularization is present in the theses in a similar manner to that in Karl Barth, but it sensibly diverges from that of Taubes. For Barth as for the next 'theological dialectics', the condition for reopening the historical process to redemption lies precisely in the fact that the world becomes 'exclusively world'. Only when the world becomes only world – only when that which can become mundane becomes completely *verweltlicht* – only then will the prospect of true redemption reappear. Benjamin's problem, from this point of view, would be that of the 'false idols' that appear within the general frame of secularization but certainly not the process of secularization as such. This is the fundamental point, in a certain sense touched upon by Taubes, but without drawing out its more radical conclusions.

Image and Ideal

The decisive theme that emerges at this point is that of nihilism as a method of worldwide policy. In Benjamin this theme is constituted in diametrical opposition not only to the apologetics of Progress but the rhetoric of 'future generations' as well. This is an absolutely explosive position with respect to the ethical revival that seemingly characterizes – on both sides of the Atlantic – current academic debates in philosophy. It is precisely in the name of the rights of future generations that the 'pyramids of sacrifice' were created in the course of Western history. It is in the name of the rights of an ill-defined Future that we have sacrificed present lives to fabricate paradise on Earth. One thinks of the epitaph-like sentence that concludes thesis XII: the 'Hatred' and 'spirit of sacrifice' of the oppressed classes 'are nourished by the image (*Bild*) of enslaved ancestors, rather than by the ideal (*Ideal*) of liberated grandchildren'.[6] The strength of the symbol – the *Bild*, as contrasted with the *Ideal* – is therefore rooted in the past, not in the future of the philosophy of history. I am not maintaining that what is at stake here is *sic et simpliciter* the problem of political messianism, nor is it the relationship between the messianic and the political in the conventional sense of these terms. Rather, at stake is the theme of the Messiah: what the *Bild* of the Messiah could represent in an epoch that is at once post-religious and post-secular. A preliminary note from which to begin, so as to avoid misunderstanding the text, is that (unlike in Taubes' eschatology) here the Messiah can appear *at any moment*. It is on this point that it is difficult to deny the congruence between Benjamin's perspective and the Hebrew tradition. The *Mashîah* present in the rabbinical tradition can appear at any moment; his way is not prepared by any *plenitudo temporum*, any eschatological 'fullness of time', or an apocalyptic 'end of time'. The Hebrew Messiah is a human figure, very human – 'created by men'. Even if the Messiah, as an event, is already fixed in the original act of creation, his coming occurs in a human way: 'created by men'. Isaiah 60:22 reads: 'it will happen in its own time'. In the same verse, however, we also find, as an apparent contrast, the affirmation: 'In its time I will speed it up'. But how is it possible to speed up an event that is predetermined *ab originibus*?

The key point, on closer inspection, is that only Action can fulfill the Origin: thus the delectably Jewish paradox by which the fulfillment of the Origin is always finalized after and never before. In playing with this interwoven paradox – an originary moment in the hands of messianic action and an image of the future in which each and every instant is opportune (and which can be 'sped up') – Benjamin gambles that this acceleration should be properly considered historical and not meta-historical. Not in the sense, therefore, of history as an addition, but rather history as a *constellation* open to *Erlösung* (a category imported from the lexicon of Franz Rosenzweig that is implicitly distinct – symbolically and semantically – from the notion of *Rettung*).

The Messiah can come any day. Every generation deposits within itself its own particular terminus: its own peculiar *kairós*, hidden but ready to be revealed at any instant – we just don't know when. A number of scholars within the Hebrew tradition, such as Sadya Gahòn and others, have tried to compute the date for the *Kétz*, the expiration of the Messiah. I believe, on the other hand, that Maimonides was right when, in *Principles of Faith*, he affirmed: 'I believe with complete faith in the coming of the Messiah. Even if he may be late, I await him every day – any day until he will arrive'. The word 'any' is very important. This is precisely the Hebrew orientation that we find in Benjamin. We only have to establish: in what form? In what conceptual configuration? In what interweaving of the theoretical and practical?

End Times

The explanatory key is provided by the thesis numbered XVIII[7] in the important typeset version of *Über den Begriff der Geschichte,* which has been rediscovered by Giorgio Agamben. This is a crucial thesis whose trajectory outlines a decline in messianism exactly in the direction we have already stressed. 'In the idea of classless society', Benjamin affirms in the opening of the thesis, 'Marx secularized the end of messianic time'. And right afterwards he adds: 'And that was a good thing'. The degeneration occurs later, at the moment when the ideological vision of the workers' social democratic movement effects a kind of sublimation of *Vorstellung* into *Ideal*: 'It was only when the Social Democrats elevated this idea to an "ideal" that the trouble began'.[8]

The scale tips in the direction of a 'deactivation' of the messianic-political charge with the neo-Kantian doctrine of the 'infinite task' (which became *Schulphilosophie*, the 'scholarship' of the Social Democratic Party, Benjamin specifies, with intellectuals and directors like Robert Schmidt, August Stadler, Paul Natorp, and Karl Vorländer). Once the end of a society without classes was defined as an asymptotic movement oriented towards an ideal scheme, 'the empty and homogeneous time was transformed into an anteroom, so to speak, in which one could wait for the emergence of the revolutionary situation with greater or lesser equanimity'.[9] The passive character of the wait is not therefore a prerogative of the messianic but rather of a transcendental and undifferentiated concept of historical time incapable of seizing the at once singular and 'vertebrate' constellation of the present. Continuing on in the same thesis we find the theme of the 'moment' (*Augenblick*). It has by now been clarified, thanks to the scholarly exegesis of the last few years, that the category of *Augenblick* carries, within the theses, a function distinct from that of *Jetztzeit* (of the 'now' or the 'now-time'). Why, then, in this crucial passage of the theses, does he speak about *Augenblick* and not *Jetztzeit*: about a moment and not about the time of the now? In my opinion, there can be but one plausible reply: only if we act to speed up the coming can revolutionary action be properly defined as messianic. However, here lies the decisive element, every point, every monad of historical time is susceptible and, if adequately rooted in the concept, can be transformed into the messianic time of the end (*Messianische Endzeit*). But let's go directly to the text:

> In reality, there is not a moment that would not carry with it *its* revolutionary chance – provided only that it is defined in a specific way, namely as the chance for a completely new resolution of a completely new problem [*Aufgabe*]. For the revolutionary thinker, the peculiar revolutionary chance offered by every historical moment gets its warrant from the political situation. But it is equally grounded, for this thinker, in the right of entry which the historical moment enjoys vis-à-vis a quite distinct chamber of the past, one which up to that point has been closed and locked. The entrance into this chamber coincides in a strict sense with political action, and it is by the means of such entry that political action, however destructive, reveals itself as messianic.[10]

The Moment of Danger

Reinterpreted in light of this crucial passage of the theses, Benjamin's messianism gains a new and more intense sense. More precisely, it is placed at the intersection between the moment (*Augenblick*) and the past (*Vergangenheit*), outside of the 'future-oriented' symbolism of waiting. Every instant carries within it the *enérgeia*, the power (*potentia*) or virtuality of the messianic: on the condition that it be conceptualized – *begriffen*, literally: caught, ensnared – in its singular, unrepeatable specificity. It is only when political action can be recognized as messianic action that *Jetztzeit* is converted into *Augenblick*. But there is more to it. The constellations of the 'now-time' are converted into the 'moment' not by virtue of a utopian tension in the direction of the future, but because of the fact that the memory (*Erinnerung*) of the past of the oppressed – as indicated in thesis VI – 'flashes up at a moment of peril' (*'im Augenblick einer Gefahr aufblitz'*).[11] It is in the image of the past therefore and not in some 'projection' of the future that one finds the key to the reciprocal conversion of messianism and historical materialism: 'Historical Materialism wishes to retain that image of the past [*Bild der Vergangenheit*] which unexpectedly appears to man singled out by history at a moment of danger'. It is in that unpredictable and unexpected 'flash' that revolutionary action comes to the fore, and it is precisely in that moment that we find ourselves in the time properly called messianic.[12] Yet if the messianic is not in the proper sense the time of waiting, it is also not mere *Jetztzeit*. The monadic density of *Nunc*, of the present, of the now, is the subject of the 'interpreter', of the historian capable of seizing the constellation determined by the present in its *Darstellung*. Messianic time is rather a time of action, because only through acting do we become revolutionary subjects, subjects capable of effecting a conversion from the 'political' into the 'messianic'.

Messianic Action

At this point, however, things become even more complicated, and it is necessary to reorient the matter. Redemption, which we are able to reactivate through action, is (as we have seen) tied to the flash of the image of the past. And, once again, the bifocal correlation of the twin axes messianism/historical materialism produces, in thesis XIV, a secret symmetry of opposites: at one pole we find the 'tiger's leap into the past' (*Tigersprung ins Vergangene*) represented by fashion (on this subject we know how Benjamin related modernity and fashion through his reading of Georg Simmel); on the other side we find the dialectic leap (*dialektischer Sprung*). One must here observe how between these two 'leaps' there is at the same time an analogy and a contrast, a sort of conflicting affinity. Fashion's leap into the past, with its 'flair for the topical, no matter where it stirs in the thickets of long ago', certainly captures the dimension of the *Jetztzeit*, extracting it from the historicist continuum of 'homogeneous and empty time'; and in a sense the French Revolution, in the same person of Robespierre, 'evoked ancient Rome the way fashion evokes the continuum of history'. Yet this leap occurs, inevitably, in a space already predisposed and prefigured by power, 'in an area where the ruling class gives the commands'. On the other hand, in spite of any structural analogy, this is radically different from the way in which the continuum of Progress explodes as a result of the dialectical jump in the Marxian concept of revolution. The categorical referent of this leap is no longer the now-time but precisely the Now, an *Augenblick* that thesis XV – in confirmation of what has been argued – intimately fuses with the dimension of action: 'The awareness that they are about go make the continuum of history explode is characteristic of the evolutionary class at the moment of their action'.[13]

At this crossroads one finds Benjamin's original re-elaboration of the theme of the 'state of exception' (*Ausnahmezustand*), understood – with and against Carl Schmitt – as a theft of the homogenous, empty time which culminated in a continuum of self-referential domination and produced, as a *very modern* phenomenon, the horror of fascism. Despite all the 'mythologies of legitimation' of Romantic derivation, the essence of fascism does not reside in a nostalgic recourse to the past but is inscribed in the technocratic power (*potenza*) that one attributes to the modern concept of progressive history. From this point of view, for Benjamin progress feeds fascism exactly as it feeds the worker's movement, which in that continuum has passively slackened its pace: 'Nothing has corrupted', one reads in thesis XI, 'the German working class so much as the notion that it was moving with the current. It regarded technological developments as the fall of the stream with which it thought it was moving'.[14]

The Secularized Abyss of the Cosmos

But how does one escape this impasse, this entropic derivative of the historical process? One escapes, for Benjamin, not only by exploding this continuum through the steep point of convergence between historical materialism and messianism but also by detaching oneself from the anthropocentric roots common to all traditional forms of messianism and the ideological variants (whether progressivist or revolutionary) that have 'secularized' it. From this point of view, the allusion to Blanqui's *L' Éternité par les Astres* is decisive. What precisely is the strategic importance of this work for Benjamin? Blanqui provides not only the idea of a 'secularized abyss' with his image of the cosmos (as we find written in the material on *Passagenwerk*); he actually illustrates how the messianic idea – coinciding with the syncope, the acceleration of time – is one and the same with the knowledge that the entire history of *Homo sapiens* is but a fragment, an infinitesimal segment when viewed against the whole of cosmic time. The apocalyptic shortening of time is flipped in this way from an indicator of centrality and absoluteness into a figure of the finitude and brevity of human history. The theme of accelerating time appears, as is well known, in Luther's *Table Talk* inside a suggestive representation of the imminence of the apocalypse as a vertiginous shortening of time, whereby centuries become years, months become weeks, weeks turn into days, days into hours, hours into minutes, and minutes become seconds: *Dann die Welt eilet davon, quia per hoc decennium vere novum saeculum fuit.*[15]

Benjamin's symbolic inversion consists in making this unheard syncopation of time the figure of absolute contingency in human history. Benjamin introduces, therefore, an anti-anthropocentric tendency in all traditional visions of history (be they progressive or revolutionary): none of which is capable of thinking through the 'strangeness' and 'disorientation' that surrounds, and relativizes, the events of History and Civilization.

Violence and Redemption

This theme brings us, moving towards a conclusion, to a further motif: taking this cosmic 'disorientation' as a starting point, how does one identify the space or opening produced by the convergence of messianism and historical materialism? We know that such an opening is very narrow, what Benjamin calls a 'strait gate' (*kleine Pforte*) through which the Messiah might enter. The strait gate represents the precariousness of a *dangerously minimal margin*. The Messiah does not arrive as the grand representation of Roman Catholicism, as Schmitt thought, but appears in a moment of danger, when a small opening seems to reveal itself: the entryway for the messianic is also the entrance point of contingency, of transience. The entrance point is a contingency that is 'kairological'and that coincides with a sort of interlude between being and nothingness, 'fullness' and 'emptiness', and desperation and hope.

Thus Benjamin draws from Auguste Blanqui the ideas of contingency and of nature as an eschatological category. He makes them intersect at the point where the dangerously minimal character of the margin and the opening to redemption are caught in a precarious equilibrium. One finds in this precarious equilibrium the theoretical traces of Marx. But this Marx is not the 'halved' Marx of tradition, nor the 'scientist' Marx of explanation (seeking to describe the laws of movement of capital); it is not even the 'prophet' Marx of historico-dialectical narrative (mytho-poetically intent on inspiring the energies of the revolutionary subject). Rather, it is the Marx of *Darstellung*, capable of fusing, in an explosive synthesis, the 'spectroscopic' analysis of a world dominated by commodity fetishism with the latent messianic tension in every authentically revolutionary action. In this way, the Marxist representation is transformed in the Benjaminian laboratory into the essential chemical reagent necessary for a synthesis of science and redemption. And it is in virtue of this fusion that the phantasmagoric analysis of commodities (re-read by Benjamin in almost surrealist terms) is permeated with a pathos that originates in the 'experience' (*Erfahrung*) of the oppressed, of the defeated – or, to use a suggestive expression by Primo Levi, the 'submerged' of history. Once invested with an appeal to the past, the historical-materialist *Darstellung* is capable of restoring the constellation of a present open to messianic action (diametrically opposed to the apologetic *Vorstellung* of a present sealed by the mythology and jurisprudence of the victor).

We Are the Expected

Here blossoms the truly conclusive aspect of Benjamin's political messianism: it corresponds to the past's appeal rather than an injunction of the future. A radical and symbolic inversion of the notion of the 'messianic wait' departs from this, making the present generation – *every* present generation – the recipients or 'object' of the wait and the 'subject' of redemption. In short, *we are the ones the dead are 'waiting for'*. The extraordinary emphasis of thesis II can have no other meaning:

> The past carries with it a temporal index by which it is referred to redemption. There exists a secret agreement between past generations and the present one. ... Like every generation that preceded us, we have been endowed with a *weak* messianic power, a power to which the past has a claim.[16]

It is we, then, we who live in the present, who are invested by past generations with the responsibility, not to safeguard a utopian hope or wait but to engage

State of Exception 33

in messianic action. Once transcribed as 'the flash in a moment of danger' of a past that has not been redressed for the oppressed, for the victims and those without name, the Benjaminian idea of redemption merges with the feeling that 'even the dead will not be safe from the enemy.' if that enemy continues to win.[17]

The return, in the heart of the text, to the cabbalistic theme of redemption as an unsaturated formula, as with the Jewish paradox for which only we can save God, occurs therefore from the dissolution of a concept of history oriented towards a linear 'homogenous and empty time'. And still, something of the linearity remains: precisely in the feeling of an irreversibility declined, *à la* Baudelaire, in hyper-modern key: from the moment we find ourselves irreversibly thrust onto an *'Einbahnstrasse'*, a one-way street, it is not the beginning but the end that is at stake for the Angel of History.

To paraphrase Kafka (another key author for comprehending Benjamin's latent sense of messianism-without-delay): faced with the messianic appeal of a past of which we – we who live in the constellation of the *Jetztzeit* – are the sole destination and heirs, what matters is not the road but the end, the terminal point. *That which we call the road is nothing but our own hesitation.*

Notes

1 For a 'genealogical' reconstruction of the philosophical and political-theological questions implied by 'Säkularisierungs theorem', please see my: *Potere e secolarizzazione. Le categorie del tempo* (1983), new extended edition, Bollati Boringhieri, Torino 2005; German edition, with updated bibliography *Macht und Säkularisierung. Die Kategorie der Zeit*, Verlag Neue Kritik, Frankfurt am Main 1989; *Cielo e terra. Genealogia della secolarizzazione* Laterza, Roma-Bari 1994; German edition revised and extended, *Die Säkularisierung der westlichen Welt*, Insel, Frankfurt am Main 1996.

2 Theodor W. Adorno and Walter Benjamin, *Briefwechsel. 1928–1940*, ed., Henri Lonitz, Suhrkamp, Frankfurt am Main 1994, p. 442.

3 Cfr. Benjamin, *Über den Begriff der Geschichte*, GS, I-2, p. 697.

4 Cfr. Jacob Taubes, *Walter Benjamin–ein moderner Marcionit? Scholems Benjamin-Interpretation religionsgeschichtlich überprüft*, in: *Antike und Moderne. Zu Walter Benjamins "Passagen,"* ed. Norbert Bolz und Richard Faber, Königshausen & Neumann, Würzburg 1986, pp. 138–147.

5 Cfr. Michele Ranchetti "Preface" to Jacob Taubes, *Escatologia occidentale*, ed. Elettra Stimilli, Garzanti, Milano 1997, pp. 7–15.

6 W. Benjamin, *Über den Begriff der Geschichte*, p. 700.

7 Cfr. W. Benjamin, *Sul concetto di storia* eds., Gianfranco Bonola and Michele Ranchetti, Einaudi, Torino 1997, pp. 52–55. In this edition the thesis in question has been inserted under the number XVIIa 'so as not to disturb the established numbering of *GS*, which has already been adopted by scholars' [see the editors's note, 19]).

8 Ibid., p. 52 [Das Unheil setzt damit ein, daß die Sozialdemokratie diese Vorstellung zum 'Ideal' erhob].

9 Ibid., p. 54 [so verwandelte sich die leere und homogene Zeit sozusagen in ein Vorzimmer, in dem man mit mehr oder weniger Gelassenheit auf den Eintritt der revolutionären Situation warten konnte].

10 Ibid. [In Wirklichkeit gibt es nicht einen Augenblick, der *seine* revolutionäre Chance nicht mit sich führt – sie will nur als eine spezifische begriffen sein, nämlich als Chance einer ganz neuen Lösung vorgeschrieben von einer ganz neuen Aufgabe. Dem revolutionären Denker bestätigt sich die eigentümliche revolutionäre Chance aus einer gegebenen politischen Situation heraus. Aber sie bestätigt sich ihm nicht minder durch die Schlüsselgewalt eines Augenblicks über ein ganz bestimmtes, bis dahin verschlossenes Gemach der Vergangenheit. Der Eintritt in dieses Gemach fählt mit der politischen Aktion strikt zusammen; und er ist es, durch den sie sich, wie vernichtend immer, als eine messianische zu erkennen gibt].

11 Benjamin, *Über den Begriff der Geschichte*, p. 695.

12 Ibid.

13 Ibid., p. 701 [Das Bewußtsein, das Kontinuum der Geschichte auf zusprengen, ist den revolutionären Klassen im Augenblick ihrer Aktion eigentümlich].

14 Ibid., p. 698.

15 Martin Luther, *Tischreden*, in *Werkausgabe*, II, p. 2756 b. See Giacomo Marramao, *Macht und Säkularisierung*, cit., p. 92 ff.

16 Benjamin, *Über den Begriff der Geschichte*, pp. 693–694.

17 Ibid., p. 695.

4 Interlude

The Other Side of the Mirror: Sovereign *Dépense* – The Scandal of the Gift

Gift and Exchange

What is the gift? What role can a philosophical consideration on the gift play today, in a world that appears increasingly governed by exchange, by the logic of profit and by the individualistic-acquisitive rationality of a *Homo oeconomicus* intent on modelling his own choices on the optimization of the cost–benefit calculation? And in what sense, with respect to what, does the dimension (and the practice) of the gift literally represent a *scandal*, introducing a factor of *incommensurability* into the system of human relationships?

To attempt an answer to these questions, it is first of all necessary to draw clear lines of demarcation. To say something new, or simply further, on the category of the gift is, in fact, extremely difficult, after the research of a great anthropologist like Marcel Mauss and the uses that have been made of it on the one hand by Georges Bataille, with his theory of *dépense* (of 'unproductive expenditure'), for the other by Karl Polanyi, with his anthropological-economic critique of the notion of 'self-regulated market', and after the resumption of their theses by Marshall Sahlins and the group of the *Mouvement Anti-Utilitariste dans le Sciences Sociales (M.A.U.S.S.)*, led by Alain Caillé and Serge Latouche, or by Marcel Hénaff and philosophers such as Jacques Derrida, Jean-Luc Nancy, Paul Ricoeur, and Jean-Luc Marion.

In dealing with the questions of the gift of Mauss – and of sovereignty as *dépense*, surplus, excess, and unproductive expenditure, of Bataille – we have made, with respect to the previous chapter, a passage from the themes of the Frankfurt Critical Theory to those of another relevant group intellectual, represented by the Parisian College of Sociology. Founded in 1937 by Georges Bataille and Roger Caillois, with the participation of Michel Leiris and other prominent exponents of Parisian intellectuality, the *Collège de Sociologie* carried out its activity with the famous conferences held every two weeks in a bookshop in the Latin Quarter, until the summer of 1939. These are dramatic years preceding the Second World War, when the disappointments of democracy and the advance of totalitarianism push this group of radical intellectuals on the road to a 'sacred sociology'. However, despite the name, it was

DOI: 10.4324/9781032632827-4

a sociological analysis not limited to the study of religious institutions but extended to all social aggregations, captured at their points of intersection not only with community aggregations but also with individual psychology. It is no coincidence that the first meeting between Bataille and Caillois takes place at Jacques Lacan. And it is no coincidence that, alongside psychoanalysis, the Collège's other great interest is particularly directed towards cultural anthropology and Marcel Mauss' theory of the gift.[1]

The famous essay by Georges Bataille 'La Notion de Dépense', published in January 1933 in Boris Souvarine's review 'La Critique sociale', draws direct inspiration from the category of 'potlatch', which – derived from a comparison between the ethnological researches of Franz Boas and Bronislaw Malinowski – is at the center of Marcel Mauss' *Essai sur le don* (1923). And yet, in taking up this strange sort of gift, understood as a form of exchange 'without counterpart' capable of constituting the true, authentic glue of the community, Bataille develops it in terms of an 'unproductive dépense', an unproductive expenditure, which opens up the possibility of a 'general economy', which represents the specular reverse of the paradigm of rational calculation and of the 'profit' on which political economy had modelled the figure of *Homo economicus*.[2]

The outcome of this project, on which Bataille will work for over 15 years, is represented by *La Parte maudite*, which will see the light in 1949.[3]

It is significant that, following Bataille, the motif of the 'generalized political economy' was subsequently taken up by Jean Baudrillard in his 'critique of the political economy of the sign': in the radical terms of a true and proper dissolution of the economy in a semiotic key, and in a subversion of the interminable production-consumption cycle which included the 'symbolic' and the 'sign-value'.[4]

However, the conceptual distinctions that I will introduce will aim at bringing out a decisive circumstance for me: none of the approaches outlined so far proves to be capable of grasping the *scandalous* singularity of the gift. The nature of the scandal that the dimension of the gift exhibits consists, on closer inspection, in its double irreducibility: not only with respect to 'selfish' behaviours but with respect to 'altruistic' behaviours themselves. In short, it is a question of understanding that, by virtue of its uniqueness, the gift is placed beyond the classical antithesis of selfishness and altruism. But let's proceed in order, focusing, in successive passages, on the lines of demarcation that separate the gift from the other dimensions to which it has been – implicitly or explicitly, unconsciously and intentionally – brought back.

One of the current definitions of the gift can be summed up in the formula of 'priceless exchange'. The gift would thus be the guiding criterion of the economy of the 'third sector', based on solidarity and voluntary work and *prima facie* opposed to the economy in the strict sense: to the 'acquisitive' dimension that characterizes the economic sphere in the modern age. In this way, the gift coincides with the complex of 'no profit' activities. It does everything that the profit-driven economy cannot. It welds the bonds of solidarity, acting as the community glue of society: the glue, the deep, subcutaneous, connective tissue that simple exchange relationships are unable to produce. However, put in these terms, the notion of the gift doesn't occupy a really 'other' space: it's not actually placed outside the economic exchange. On the contrary, it constitutes its premise and embryonic form.

Despite the extraordinary richness and complexity of his analytic construct, the tendency to establish a continuum between gift and exchange is discernible, on closer inspection, precisely in Mauss' *Essai sur le don.* The gift implies a triple obligation: give–receive–repay. However, the geometry designed by the obligatory movement of giving is twofold. It can be linear or circular: developing along the axial relationship of reciprocity (gift–counter–gift) or taking the form of a temporally deferred return, as in the backwards parabola of a boomerang. Although he characterizes the gift as an all-encompassing social phenomenon, Mauss sees in its counterpart obligation the prefiguration of more complex and evolved market systems: the 'custom of exchanging gifts', in other words, would be the hallmark of societies that have have left behind the system of 'total performance' but have not yet reached the 'individual contract stage' with the actual trading, pricing, and minting of money. The gift therefore presents itself as an archaic prefiguration of exchange and as a factor of neutralization of the potential conflict present in societies built on a system of parental alliances and solidarity. The leitmotif that can be enucleated from this thesis has a wide circulation in French anthropology of the last century: even Claude Lévi-Strauss, despite criticizing Mauss, sees in the familiar forms of the exchange of gifts the primary structural principle of society.

Symbolic Violence

But once placed in relation to the exchange, the gift inevitably ends up losing any alternative or liberating connotation, to present itself as an expression of that phenomenon which for Pierre Bourdieu comes to be placed in the sphere of 'symbolic violence'. The logic of obligations, centred on the credit–debt pair, as the creator of a 'symbolic capital', is the 'cheaper system of domination'. The gift is therefore the constitutive dimension of a power enclosed in the act of giving itself: of a credit power that is acquired by giving. His device is far from uneconomical: on the contrary, it represents the primary scene of the modern economic system. Consequently, pre-capitalist communities cannot be nostalgically idolized as romantic examples of cooperative, harmonious, and violence-free civilizations.

Thus, we witness the emergence of a decisive implication of the gift-exchange nexus. The reductionist flattening implicit in the obligatory and

cogent device attributed by anthropology to the ritual practices of 'donation' therefore invests the two forms – the reciprocal form and the circular
form – of the gift, highlighted some time ago by the writer and *Kulturkritiker*
Lewis Hyde in a book entitled, as will be seen, truly symptomatic: *The Gift:
Imagination and the Erotic Life of Property.*[5] The reduction is not limited
only to the axial form of the gift, which not only constitutes it as a symmetrical relationship of reciprocity but also fully involves its circular form.
In other words: the obliging function is not performed solely, as Hyde seems
to believe, by the 'constrictive reciprocity' but by the circular movement of
the gift within the overall structure of the society. Moreover, it is precisely the
symbolic efficacy of this ritual interaction which, by making all members of
the society responsible for maintaining relationships, constitutes the true glue
of the community bond.

But in what sense does the circular shape of the gift reduce its paradoxical significance, neutralizing its 'scandalous' character? Shouldn't asserting
the symbolic nature of the gift, as I have just done, imply its irreducibility to
the economic logic of exchange, proper to the utilitarian paradigm? Clearly,
this is another crucial step. A step that imposes a further level of radicality in the analysis and conceptual distinctions. In an important consideration
of the relationship between 'gift' and 'symbolism', contained in the volume
The third paradigm, Alain Caillé affirmed that, with his *Essay on the Gift*,
Mauss would have 'laid the foundations of an alternative and complementary paradigm at the same time to the two dominant paradigms in the social
sciences – methodological individualism and holism': this paradigm could
be qualified as the 'paradigm of the gift, of symbolism and of the Political'.
Such an extremely demanding formulation 'implies that between gift, symbolism and politics (in the sense of the Political and not of politics) there
exists a kind of identity, of profound analogy, of isomorphism or, at least, of
coextensiveness'.[6]

One aspect stands out, in the first place, from the isomorphism that
is detected by Caillé between gift, symbol, and the Political (correctly
distinguished from politics). If, on the one hand, isomorphism excludes
that perfect reciprocity which cancels the gift, flattening it eo ipso on the
exchange, on the other it enhances its perfect circular functionality as a
feeder of the social order. This order certainly has to do with the dimension of the 'Political'. But the political order, understood as the symbolic
glue of the social bond, is anything but extraneous or unrelated to the logic
of the economy. To illustrate the meaning and implications of this aspect,
it will suffice to refer to the etymology of 'symbol'. The term which,
derived from the Greek *syn-ballein*, refers to the act of bringing together
the two halves of a coin; an act which acts as the medium of a friendship
or exchange relationship; as a means of recognition of two distant friends
who meet again (the *tessera hospitalitatis*); or – as noted, among others,
by Paul Gilbert – as a mark for the execution of a commercial procedure;

the seller who in ancient times shipped goods attached a piece of card to it, entrusting the other piece to a trustee who was supposed to show it to the buyer to collect the agreed sum.

Surplus State

The original meaning of the term 'symbol' is, therefore, far from extraneous to the economic dimension of exchange. Despite the change of its physical body in today's international trade system, the symbol continues to maintain, in the form of the contract and in the credit institution, in all respects its original function of annulling the temporal distance between the shipment of goods and payment.

In what sense, then, can we speak of the gift as a 'surplus state', according to the well-known definition of Jacques Godbout? In the sense, as Mauss had already clearly explained, of that postponement or that periodic suspension of the ordinary and routine time represented by festivities. But who could deny that the surplus represented by holidays and parties is also in all respects functional at the time of the economy? It is true that only with the process of rationalization established in modernity has the imperative of productivity increasingly extended and perfected itself, leading to a generalized domination of the economy: while in pre-modern societies – as observed by Bataille, but as he had grasped the same Marx in his analysis of the forms that precede capitalist production – the aspect of 'dissipation' prevailed. Only that unproductive expenditure performed in those societies – as indeed in our post-industrial hypermodernity – a function that was not at all liberating and in no way detached from the 'government of bodies and souls'. On the contrary, it expressed, as Pierre Bourdieu precisely observed, a coefficient that is all the higher the more subtle and indirect of 'symbolic violence'.

To take a further step towards identifying the scandal of the gift, we must therefore not lose sight of the ambivalence of its excess character, of its 'surplus nature': that is, its ambiguous nature of *dósis pharmakou*, of 'gift' and 'poison' at the same time (semantic ambivalence still present in the German *Gift*). And a conspicuous 'dose of poison' is present not only in the symmetrical gift that prefigures the exchange, but – according to an acute notation by Jean Starobinski – in the same asymmetrical gift: in all those forms of donation which, from charitable generosity to almsgiving and patronage, do not ask to be reciprocated precisely because they gratify the conscience or exalt the power of the 'donor'. On the other hand, the scandal of the gift is not captured by that other – certainly more radical or nobler – rupture of the relationship of reciprocity and symmetry envisaged by the sovereignty of Bataille's *dépense* (expenditure, unproductive waste) or by Derrida's absolute gratuitousness. In both cases, the incommensurability of the gift flattens into a limit-concept of a nihilistic-existential order (eroticism and the Nietzschean

'Self love', in Bataille) or an ethical-transcendental one (the gift not recognized as such and invisible and silent forgiveness, in Derrida).

In reality, in both cases, we are not dealing with a real break but with the 'back of the glove'of the logic of functionality and exchange.

Incommensurabiliy: The Gift as an Event

To focus on the scandal of the gift, it is therefore necessary to take a final step: seeing at work in the form of exchange a device for the *neutralization of the relationship*, of the potential enclosed in intersubjective relational practices, functional to the affirmation of the identity logic of indifference and equivalence. But if the exchange is neutralizing with respect to the relationship understood as a concrete, bodily determined dynamic of bringing irreducible singularities and differences into play, equally neutralizing will necessarily be the gift understood as its static, specular – and, therefore, anything but scandalous – reverse.

The gift is not a utopia nor an ontological-existential authenticity. It's an impossible. But an impossible that is given, that happens. It's an *Event*. But an event that takes place in a non-place: in that *metaxú*, in that *infra*, in that interlude that is located between the dimensions of the economy and ethics, between the *ratio* of productive–unproductive exchange and the functional surplus of expenditure and absolute gratuity. It is along that borderline, through that mobile area of tensions, that the gift is experienced daily as a practice of relationships in which the constitution of singularities goes hand in hand with the dismissal of individualistic mythologies.

Making the incommensurability of the gift dynamic, positively declining its irreducibility to the dimensions of the economy and ethics, would mean reversing the entropic drift of our present. It would mean giving voice and form to singularities and their relationships, making them active subjects of change.

It would basically mean: rediscovering, redefining, and re-enchanting politics.

Notes

1   As is known, the positions of Bataille and other members of the college have been accused of ambiguity by various parties and, probably, viewed with suspicion by Walter Benjamin himself, after having attended some seminars. However, it should be remembered that the *Passages* dossier (the project of the great work the great work to which Benjamin was devoting himself at the end of his life) was hidden and kept in the Bibliothèque Nationale thanks to Bataille. For a large collection of texts and materials on the College's activities, see the volume *Le Collège de Sociologie (1937–1939)*, ed. by Denis Hollier, Gallimard, Paris 1979.

2   See now the new edition of "La Notion de Dépense", Nouvelles Éditions Lignes, Paris 2011.

3   G. Bataille, *La Parte maudite*, Éditions de Minuit, Paris 1949.

4 See J. Baudrillard, *Pour une critique de l'économie politique du signe* [1972], English Translation, *For a Critique of the Political Economy of the Sign*, Telos Press, St. Louis 1981; Id., "When Bataille Attacked the Metaphysical Principle of Economy", D.J. Miller (trans.), *Canadian Journal of Political and Social Theory*, Vol. 11, 1987, pp. 57–62.
  For an overall reconstruction of Baudrillard's intellectual path – philosophical and transdisciplinary – see now the extensive, highly documented and 'testimonial' book by Serge Latouche, *Remember Baudrillard*, Fayard, Paris 2019.
5 Lewis Hyde, *The Gift: Imagination and the Erotic Life of Property*, Random House, New York 1983.
6 A. Caillé, *Anthropologie du don. Le tiers paradigme*, Desclée de Brouwer, Paris 2000.

5 Easts and Wests

'Auctoritas' and 'Potestas': The Sacred Space of the Political

Various and innumerable ideas *reçues* crowd into the theological–political debate today around the endiads *auctoritas/potestas* and sacred/profane. An 'untimely meditation' on the present condition and destiny of the West and Europe in the global era cannot therefore take place except along the line between different disciplinary languages: from history to sociology, from psychology to linguistics, and from economics to cultural anthropology.

However, it would be doomed to remain on the phenomenological or merely descriptive plane should it be carried out without involving the philosophical dimension. Indeed, only from philosophy does it open up the possibility of thinking about the future of politics and human communities in the globalized world. A future that appears to be marked by the contours of what has been authoritatively defined as a *post-Hobbesian Order*: that is, by an increasingly clear separation – post-Hobbesian or, as I prefer to call it, post-Leviathan – between the political and the state dimensions. Despite the far from linear nature of the *State-building* process, the identification between politics and the state is a specific feature of the modern era and, as such, no longer corresponds to the situation of the global age, whose dominant profiles draw a trend line that is less and less traceable to the centralist-hierarchical paradigm of sovereignty.

However, this statement does not imply the acceptance of postmodern theses, which emphasize the aspect of fragmentation and dispersion while losing sight of the new logic and *merging powers* of the globalized world. It is necessary, in this regard, to be clear: globalization is not a postmodern event but – according to a definition I proposed several years ago – *hypermodern*.[1] To borrow and integrate an expression of Anthony Giddens, globalization is both a presupposition and a consequence of modernity, and only if taken in this duplicity does it become comprehensible and conceptualizable. Today's globalization, while unquestionable in its magnitude and relevance, is but the latest, tentative chapter in a series of successive globalizations that have served as a counterpoint to the modern process of civilization. And its hypermodern character consists in the fact that it brings to the tuning fork, to its extreme

DOI: 10.4324/9781032632827-5

consequences, a field of tension that has spanned the four 'long centuries' (to borrow a felicitous expression of Giovanni Arrighi) of modernity: the tension between the principle of *worldliness* and the *principle of territoriality*.

If this premise is accepted, no diagnosis of the present can take place without focusing on three aspects: the question of the *new global space*, within a general reflection on the function that spatiality plays in politics and law; the situation of Europe in the global age; and the prospects of European politics and citizenship in the globalized world. A large part of the exposition will be devoted above all to a 'genealogical' reconstruction of the first aspect, relating to the question of the new global space: an essential aspect for focusing on the still neuralgic knot that Europe represents in the 'spiritual situation' of our time. In the second section I will attempt to project the elements derived from the genealogy onto current perspectives.

Why is the issue of spatiality important today for understanding the question of the nexus between politics, law, and power? There is a famous thesis, dating back to *Der Nomos der Erde* (perhaps Carl Schmitt's most important work, published in 1950, at the centre of the tragic and extraordinary century we have behind us), which states that *nomos*, i.e. the ordering law, implies – as etymologically interconnected with the verb *nehmen* and the noun *Nahme*[2] – a taking possession and delimitation of space. The Greek notion of *Nomos basileus* originally refers to a *nomothesía*, that is, a synthesis of the two constitutive moments of power, without which the very possibility of understanding the essence of politics and law remains interdicted: violence and perimeter, energetics and topology. Originally, any delimitation of space is a sacred operation. But how should we first understand the sacred. The sacred is not the 'numinous', the *mysterium tremendum*, of Rudolf Otto. The sacred is, on the contrary, the epitome of Order as a circumscribed sphere, an enclosed and inviolable space (the famous 'enclosure of the sacred').

In the 1930s, the Parisian *Collège de Sociologie* had unequivocally defined the idea of the sacred: 'sacred' is a spatially perimetered social sphere, whose clauses of inclusion/exclusion, of access or prohibition, are strictly predetermined. From here, however, descended a decisive consequence: what is excluded or expelled from the perimeter of the sacred is precisely the element that characterizes its essence and determines its form. Here the theses of the *Collège de Sociologie* on the sacred as *excess* (and, as far as Bataille is concerned – as seen in the previous chapter – on the unproductive excess as a mark of sovereignty) intersect with those developed, in a theological-political key, by the Schmittian texts of the 1920s to the 1930s around the 'state of exception', the *Ausnahmezustand*: it is the exception, the excess that exceeds the spatial delimitation of law, and not the norm that constitutes the legal order and qualifies its essence.

The Schmittian utterance seems to be echoed, in a different linguistic context but within the same temperament, by Georges Bataille's expressions: it is the excess, the unproductiveness of the dispensation, not the serial and everyday industriousness of the useful, that constitutes the motive and the engine of the community. The delimitation of sacred space, in which all automatism of Order consists, could not take place without the 'cursed part': without the blind spot of its representation.

But there is more. Every sacred order is characterized by boundaries that are sharply drawn: according to the criterion of a *rectitudo* that is both geometric and moral. On the other hand, the anomic and virtually anti-nomic resistance exerted, as undialectizable negativity, by the surplus, the constitutive 'curse' of the sacred, subjects the boundary lines drawn from time to time to tension. The influential scene of the sacred thus has an inevitable consequence that ends up falling back on the same paradigm of the legal order: the idea of boundary bears within it an ambivalence that, alongside the meaning of the ultimate margin, the terminal line, recalls the sense of sharing with an excluded otherness or extraneousness. Boundary is not simply limit, but *with-end*: limit with-shared. Boundary is, on the one hand, a line of demarcation and separation: the Roman god Terminus, presiding over the demarcation of territory by means of 'terminal stones'. On the other hand, however, it implies a sharing: a commonality along the line through which the dividing furrow is drawn. The boundary is thus presented in the form of an oxymoron: a *barrier of contact* through which two antithetical polarities, the inside and the outside of the order, are partitioned and at the same time co-apparate. The etymology and semantics of the boundary thus replicate the characteristic feature of all sacredness.

The moment of *rectitudo* is essential to define the sacred order and space of right, *nomos*, and law. Linguists have long attempted to understand the original function of the term *rex* in archaic Roman times and, even earlier, of the lemma *raj-(an)* in Sanskrit. For Émile Benveniste, both terms derive from the root **reg-*, which connects the Latin *regere* to the Greek verb *orégō*, the meaning of which is 'to lay in a straight line'. The cross-reference to *orégō* is admittedly introduced with some caution by Benveniste, while it is instead radically challenged, as being only a 'bland earring', by Giovanni Semerano's etymological dictionary devoted to *The Origins of European Culture*.[3] Extending the comparison to Akkadian-Sumerian and Semitic languages, Semerano aims to dismiss Benveniste's Rex-signer hypothesis of all foundations: going so far as to assert that

the French linguist, in order to rediscover the original values of *rex* and explore the historical zones of its origins, would have had to follow an impervious path, forbidden to an Indo-Europeanist, beginning with the Homeric concept of king-shepherd of peoples, [...] to go back to the voice rējûm, rē'ûm, ancient Akkadian rā'ûm (shepherd: title of king, 'shepherd', 'leader', 'ruler').[4]

This is not the place to settle a controversy that calls into question two suggestive influential scenes of power, traceable to the regal model and the pastoral model: models jointly assumed by Foucault under the formula 'Omnes et Singulatim', as if they were two sides in tension of a single medal (*regal* government of 'all', of a collective subject included in a space, and *pastoral* leadership attentive to the individual units of which the 'flock' of the governed is composed). It suffices for us here to reiterate that Benveniste was fully aware of the possible objections to his hypothesis when he observed:

> In theory, nothing stands in the way of the possibility of connecting *rex* with gr. *orégō*; the *o-* is not in the way, it attests to an ancient initial that Latin has not preserved. The meaning of the Greek forms needs to be clarified. The present *orégō* or *orégnumi* [...] does not only mean 'to lay down'; this sense is also that of another verb, *petánnumi*. But *petánnumi is 'to spread* in the sense of width,' while *orégō, orégnumi* is 'to spread in a straight line'.[5]

The etymology of Latin *rex* is thus intertwined, through Indo-European roots, with that of Greek terms such as *areté* (virtue), *arithmos* (number as an ordering scansion), and *aristos* (the best as a mark of excellence). It is, on closer inspection, the same root from which all the Latin terms connected with the adjective *rectus* – hence the Germanic *Recht* and the English *right* – and the noun *rectitudo* are derived: to a rectitude at once ethical and geometrical. If *rex* is the *rectus* par excellence, the one who holds righteousness, then the original meaning of *rex* is not that of king or ruler, as it has been understood by moderns, but that of *rex sacrorum*: an expression that does not mean 'king of sacred things' but '*marker* of the sphere of the sacred'. The original meaning of *rex* is, therefore, that of 'marker'. Its primary function is *regere fines*, the 'marking of boundaries'. *Rex* is the agent-operator who *regit*, marks, and traces in a straight line the edges of a space. The same semantic horizon presides over the emergence of another key term of spatial ordering:

> The important word *regio* does not originally mean 'the region,' but 'the point reached in a straight line.' Thus is explained the meaning of the expression *e regione*: 'opposite,' that is, 'in a straight line, opposite.' In the language of augurs, *regio* means 'the point reached by a straight line drawn on the ground or in the sky,' then 'the space between these straight lines drawn in different directions.'[6]

The original expression *rex regit regiones does* not mean 'the king rules, or governs, the regions', but rather 'the marker marks the signs'. Consequently, the *rex* ('more similar in this to the priest than to the king in the modern sense', Benveniste clarifies) is the one who, by locating the consecrated space, draws the boundaries between inner and outer, sacred and profane, and autochthonous territory and allochthonous territory. It is difficult, at this point, to deny the analogy between the web of etymological-lexical cross-references warped

by the great French linguist's *Vocabulary of Indo-European Institutions* and
the inextricable interweaving of *Ordnung* and *Ortung*, 'ordering' and 'locali-
zation', set up by that early anticipation of the spatial turn – of the 'spatial
turn' that occurred in the age of the world become globe – represented by *Der
Nomos der Erde*. In Schmitt, too, the energy underlying the Law of the Earth
ultimately refers back to the regal-sacerdotal function of the *Nomos basileus*:
it draws the boundaries of the community by rooting the geometric and ethical
contours of Order in that *justissima tellus that* bears within itself the 'internal
measure' of justice.

But from what source does the nomothetic function of spatial delimitation derive legitimacy? To answer this we must first clarify the relationship
between two crucial functions: *regnum* and *augurium*. This relationship, as
we shall see, is by no means harmonious, but laden with tensions. The regnal
function has a potestative and normative character: it *gives shape to* space by
delimiting it. It is not, however, a self-sufficient and absolute function: the *rex*
derives, in fact, the source of legitimacy of his function as 'marker' from the
augur, that is, from the holder of the *auctoritas*. *Auctoritas* is an augural function because it has to do-as suggested by the Indo-European root *aug-*, from
which the lemma *auctor* is also directly descended-with the act of *augere*:
with an *augmentum* of the symbolic sphere of sense-giving. But, Benveniste
observes, the meaning of *augeo* – precisely insofar as it underlies two crucial
pairs of terms such as *auctor-auctoritas* and *augur-augustus* – cannot be that
of 'augmenting, making greater *some thing that already exists* [...], but the act
of producing from one's own breast; a creative act that causes something to
arise from fertile ground'.[7]

The meaning of *augurium* is therefore not that of a quantitative increase
but of a *symbolic surplus* that must from time to time give rise to a geometrically straight way of ordering things through signs. In the relationship between
auctoritas and *potestas* we find, then, the symbolic key to the functioning of
power as the original delimitation of space. Power is nothing but a surplus of
meaning that must from time to time translate into a coherent system of signs.
The translator of meaning into a system of signs is the *rex*. But the *rex* presupposes the *auctoritas* of the augur. In the later phase of the Roman system, the
function of the augur is held essentially by the magistracy: the secularized
figures of augurs in the Roman world are the magistrates. It is no coincidence
that Octavian, as soon as he ascended to power, appropriated the magistratu-
ral function, assuming the role of Rome's first magistrate-auguror. *Augustus*
is the name of the Subject who, having become *Pontifex Maximus*, is able,
precisely, to carry out the properly *pontifical* task of 'building bridges', weld-
ing in himself the distinct functions of *augurium* and *regnum*, the symbolism
of *auctoritas* and the semiotics of regal *potestas*. The orientalizing title of
imperator – appellation with an oriental flavour once assigned in republican
Rome to military leaders – represents the seal of an influential and long-last-
ing formula, hinging on the mythology of a unique and original source of the

'sacrament of power' (P. Prodi), which would unite in itself the two poles of symbolic authority and normative power of command. Not for nothing, once he assumed the 'pontifical' function, Octavian – according to the testimony of Suetonius (Suet. *Aug.* 31.1) – had all Greek and Latin prophetic books burned at the stake. With the single, significant exception of the Sibylline Books: because of their celebratory content vis-à-vis the royal *dignitas*. The consequences of this conjunction on the life of the *Res publica* are found punctually recorded, a century after Livy and Virgil, by Tacitus' ruthless disillusionment and lucid despair: 'Nothing remained of the ancient civil conscience: resigned all feeling of equality, all waited for the nods of the prince' (*Annales*, I, iv).

Magrado this – and here we touch on the salient point – between *auctoritas* and *potestas* a field of tension is always given. The normative power of spatial delimitation is effective only through recourse to the surplus of meaning of the *augurium*. To the vertical image of authority as the foundational scene of power, it is possible, therefore, to counterpose the horizontal idea-force of an authority understood as an alternative dimension to the logic of power: an authority – Luisa Muraro recently proposed, in terms in several respects convergent with theses I myself have put forward in recent years – 'oriented in a relational sense', capable of contending with power 'on the terrain of political wager'.[8]

Even in the 'vertical' paradigm, however, there persists a hiatus, an incomprehensible qualitative dieresis between *auctoritas* and *potestas*: spatial delimitation, in fact, may meanwhile serve as a decisive symbolic factor precisely insofar as it refers back to that surplus of the meaning of the *augurium* without which the phenomenon of a *naked power devoid of authority* is produced. A recurring phenomenon in the multi-millennial history of human societies and visible to the naked eye in the current phase of *transition* or *interregnum* between the no-more of the old modern inter(nation state)order and the not-yet of a new order that is struggling to emerge.[9]

The Invention of the Orient

However, there is another specific consequence of the original idea of space understood as a legal order: the distinction between border and frontier or rather between the symbolism of the border and the symbolism of the frontier. These are two different symbolisms, which we could trace back, respectively, to the territorial paradigm of a Europe understood, according to a suggestive thesis of Étienne Balibar, as a continent of borders, of Europe shaped by the *civil law* tradition and centred on the towering concept of 'sovereignty'; and, on the other hand, that is, to the frontier and *common law* countries' tradition, to the West as a deterritorializing 'drift', as a continuous shifting of the limit. The symbolisms of border and frontier both belong, *pleno iure*, to the genetic code of European culture. In the developments of the idea of Europe, however, it is possible to detect a progressive derubrication of the theme of the frontier towards the theme of the border. From its origins, Europe poses itself as the country of the frontier, *not* of the border, and it elaborates a symbolic device that presents itself, *in nuce*, constitutive of the very idea of the West: an idea coined from its earliest beginnings in tandem with its *alter ego* Orient. The East–West endiad is a dualism wholly internal to the West. A binary schema from which has been produced, over the centuries, the 'Orientalist' stereotype stigmatized in now-classical terms by Edward Said and, along its track, by postcolonial authors such as Gayatri Chakravorty Spivak, Homi Bhabha, Dipesh Chakrabarty, and Arjun Appadurai (whose philosophical implications have been dealt with densely and illuminatingly by Emanuela Fornari in a book prefaced by Balibar and significantly titled *Boundary Lines: Philosophy and Postcolonialism*).[10] But several decades before Said and *postcolonial studies*, the conceptual-symbolic device of the East–West pair as a dualism internal to the West and essential to its self-identification had been highlighted by Karl Jaspers in his seminal 1949 book *Vom Ursprung und Ziel der Geschichte*. Beginning with Herodotus and Aristotle, the pair takes on the contours of a real antithesis between the productive and free West and the seductive and despotic East (think of the long *querelle* around 'Eastern despotism' that kept much of twentieth-century Marxism busy). But – and here I can only reiterate what I have already argued in my previous works[11] – the fact that Western Reason is inconceivable without that internal polarity and therefore calls into question the *necessity of* reference to the Other for the purposes of its own symbolic self-identification confers on the self-ascritical act of 'primacy' performed by the West, a significance that is not merely one of hierarchical supremacy but at the same time also one of unconscious dependence. A dependence inscribed from the very beginning in the mirror nature of the internal relationship of the East–West dyad. The 'Greek miracle' founded the world of the West: the *Abendland, the* Land of Evening, and the Land of Sunset. But, Jaspers reminds us, in such a way that the West 'continues to exist only as long as it keeps its gaze on the East, confronts it, understands it and detaches itself from it'.[12] . *Only the West* – to borrow a famous Weberian adage from the 1920 *Foreword* to Essays in the *Sociology of Religion* – feels the need to establish its own identity *per differentiam*, through an act of original decision: that is, as the very etymon of the term suggests, through a tear, a caesura, a cut (deciding is always a cutting off ...) from the supposed matrix identified in the *alter ego* 'Orient' – in the great Asian womb. It springs from here, from this inaugural myth, from this veritable 'influential scene' (to be understood precisely in the sense of Freudian *Urszene*) of our *peninsular* European identity, the specular antithesis between *productive* West and *seductive* East, *free* West and *despotic* East, and Western Frontier and Eastern Stanziality. With the inexorable contrapasso of experiencing the projection towards the Outside, the adventure of novelty and eccentricity, with the perennial anguish of being sucked into the great Asian womb: the realm of seduction and stillness, of the innermost depths and unconscious levelling. Asia is thus configured, in Jaspers' eyes, as the price of the Primacy: the *symbolic counterpoise* of a hegemony conquered through a productive Project that, directed in a linear and punctiform manner towards the expansion of the techno-scientific domination of the external world, has rendered the West constitutionally deficient and incomplete with respect to the awareness of an *other* dimension of Reason, rooted in its innermost structure and its very origin:

> While revealing the pre-eminence of the West in shaping the world, an objective historical analysis highlights at the same time its *incompleteness* and *deficiency*, which make the question concerning the East ever more timely and fruitful: what do we find there that completes us? What in it has become real, has become truth, and we instead have let slip away? What is the price of our primacy?[13]

It is worth pointing out, albeit in passing, how in this passage of the Jasperian argumentation the embryo of a thesis snaking in the anti-Heideggerian component of the *Kulturkritik* of the first half of the last century is outlined: the thesis, later developed by Habermas, of an *incompleteness of* the Modern Project not compensable through the postmodern rhetorics of drift and fragment but through the integration of the technical-instrumental side with the dialogical-discursive side of Enlightenment reason. Given the diversity of premises and theoretical referents, the analogy obligatorily stops here. And yet it appears less arbitrary if one considers Habermas' profound sharing of the Jaspersian question about the *geistige Situation der Zeit*: about a 'spiritual situation of our time' that can find a solution by reactivating a dimension of rationality that the West has so far relegated to the background, although in the last two centuries it has manifested itself at an incoactive level in some crucial passages of modern society and public sphere. For Jaspers, too, it is a matter of bringing to the surface not an alternative (or presumptively 'irrational') source of knowledge, but the removed dimension of the Logos, whose genesis is at one with the origin of *global history*: that removed which the tradition of *Subaltern Studies* would later enunciate, in a true 'hand-to-hand' with Hegel's philosophy of history established by Ranajit Guha, as the emergence of a *History at the Limit of the World-History*, of a history situated at the edge of Universal History. But, unlike Habermas, Jaspers never spoke of a 'divided West': as if a finally recomposed Western modernity could on its own, with the exclusive baggage of its Kantian-style universalism, optimally cope with dramatic global challenges. He appealed, rather, to another dimension of the *Aufklärung*, of rational 'enlightenment', which – as a radical questioning of *Dasein*, of 'situated' existence, of our being-in-the-world – shatters the mirror game between East and West, breaks through the *Western–Eastern couch* on which we have for centuries settled, revealing its secret convergence with questions from other worlds:

The realities of China and India for the past three thousand years have been pure attempts to emerge from the indeterminate Asian matrix. Emergence is a universal historical process, not a peculiar European attitude toward Asia. It takes place in Asia itself. It is the way of humanity and authentic history.[14]

Fidelity to the axis of universal history, to the convergence of the great civilizations of the planet, thus appears, at the end of Jaspers' analysis, to be the only condition for not dispersing into nothingness, in an age marked – as Paul Valéry had already grasped in the period between the wars in his extraordinary *Regards sur le monde actuel* – by a world completely saturated by the planetary extension of science and technology: a closed, accomplished world, in which there is no longer a distinction between inside and outside.[15] In this globalized world, there is no problem, action or event that does not affect the entire human race, placed at the crossroads between catastrophe and the building of a new order based on law and mutual recognition. The Jasperian conclusion thus seems to share with Heidegger, despite the radicality of the philosophical disagreement, a tragic *Leitmotiv* resulting from the Central European debate on the *globale Zeit*: in the time of global technology, the greatest opportunity for salvation lies precisely there where the danger and risk of decision have touched their extreme edge – in the *situation-limit* of possible existence. *Wo aber Gefahr ist, wächst das Rettende auch*: Hölderlin's apoftegma 'But where danger is, there also grows that which saves' would seem to be re-actualized in his eyes as well. Having said that, it should be added that the 'all-encompassing horizon' (*das Umgreifende*) represented diachronically by the axial image of civilization possesses for Jaspers the structure of a multilateral universalism, accessible only by that 'method of comparison', which today, however, cannot be limited to a resumption of the albeit grand Weberian design but must be included and surpassed in a real *politics of translation* between different histories, narratives, and forms of life.

Despite its unquestionable greatness, unsurpassed to this day, the Weberian attempt in fact presents, in cross-comparison with Jaspers' analysis, diametrically opposed limitations and advantages. The Jaspersian thesis of the 'axial age' (*Achsenzeit*), the idea of a *mysterious convergence of parallel worlds*, sustained by faith in the preordained harmony that would preside over the development of the great planetary civilizations, is matched in Weber by a tragic post-historical awareness of the *radically contingent* character of the process of secularization and 'rationalization of the world', as is evident from the splendid *incipit* of the already mentioned *Foreword* to *Religionssoziologie*: What concatenation of circumstances caused it to be precisely on the terrain of the West, and only here, that cultural phenomena were manifested which also – at least according to what we like to imagine – stood in a line of development of *universal* significance and validity?.[16] Conversely, to the self-centred limit of the Weberian comparative framework, which describes the process of rationalization and disenchantment of the world from the perspective of *a* 'West'understood as a *singularity that universalizes itself* by radiating to all other cultures, is matched in Jaspers – as we have seen – by an awareness of the *polycentric dynamic that presides over the development of civilization and rational thought*, mediated by the deconstruction of that East–West antithesis whose crystallization today constitutes the main cultural obstacle to understanding the two main epicentres of global conflict: the *antiglobalist* threat of Islamic fundamentalism and the *alternative globalization* projected by the 'geoeconomic' (even before geopolitical) ideology of the so-called 'Asian values'. Identifying the nature of these challenges is impossible without a work of decomposition capable of bringing to light the *plurality within both terms of the pair*. If we were able to accomplish such a decomposition, we would come to the surprising discovery that the polytheism of values and the multiverse of world views, which we were inclined to believe to be the exclusive preserve of the West, are also found to no lesser extent in the 'East'; that there are therefore multiple 'Easts' and multiple 'Wests' – and not all Easts necessarily in the East, and not all Wests necessarily in the West. But once the terms of the endiad have been disjointed and pluralized, it will succeed more difficult, for example, to bring Europe–Islam relations back to the supposedly symmetrical West–East antithesis: not only because, as Franco Cardini has repeatedly reminded us, the reduction of *dar al-Islam* – of the Land of faith understood as total surrender to God – to the East is now just as impractical as the biunivocal association of Christendom with Europe made in his time by Novalis; but also because, in the intercultural interweavings of the globalized world, we now have as much an Islam in the West as a West in Islam.

Western Difference and the Ghost of Freedom

But let us return to the implications of the primary scene of East–West dualism, in the knowledge that it is still an 'imagined' Origin, constructed *ex post*. Many influential studies have documented the Mesopotamian (Jean Bottéro)[17] or Afro-Asiatic roots of classical civilization (think of Martin Bernal's *Black Athena*).[18] And it would also be important to explore philosophically the fact that the two most influential trajectories of the Western tradition, represented by Athens and Jerusalem, Greekness and Judaism, both spring from a traumatic caesura with the Egyptian matrix. When we speak of *Urszene*, the influential scene or Origin, we must therefore be clear that we are dealing not with an effected historical genesis but with an embryonic form of 'self-understanding': with the self-image with which the West represents itself. In its foundational historical (Herodotus) and philosophical (Plato, Aristotle) expressions, Europe self-represents itself as an appendage, a peninsular offshoot that has detached itself from its original Asian matrix, projecting itself into the adventure of eccentricity and marginality. By no means does it understand itself as a 'Country of the Center'. Its leaning toward the Outside is a *claim to hegemony, not centrality.* Europe's original soul is maritime, not continental. Its element is the sea, not the land. Its symbolic figure is the polyvalent mobility of the frontier, not the ambivalent stability/instability of the border. We know well how important the metaphor of navigation is for European culture: the navigation of Odysseus is the influential scene of Europe and its Greek origin. But navigation is, since Plato, also the metaphor that unites philosophical proceeding with political praxis. The ship of philosophy, like the Platonic 'ship of the polis', is born under the auspices of the maritime element, not of continental rootedness (much to the chagrin of Carl Schmitt, with his claim to situate land–sea dualism in the *turning point* marked by Elizabethan England's detachment from the continent as the premise of mercantile and industrial modernity, and of Martin Heidegger, with his attempt to enclose philosophy in the forest, in the glades, in the chthonic depths, and in the heart of the earthly darkness). But – here the crucial passage – through the metaphor of navigation a biunivocal relationship is established between the West–East endiad and the freedom–dispotism pair.

Already in Herodotus we come across a clear *contrastive definition of* European identity: what characterizes 'Europeans' as opposed to 'Orientals', Ellas as opposed to Persia, Greeks as opposed to 'barbarians', is their being *demos*, a people composed of free individuals, not a mass subject to despotic rule. It is not difficult – as a liberal democratic intellectual of the stature of Norberto Bobbio noted in his time – to discern in the symbolic device of the freedom-despotism antithesis the influential scene of that 'European ideology' which, transmitted to the Atlantic West, has coined in recent years the formula of 'exporting democracy'. The marker of *Western difference* is, on closer inspection, deposited in a concept that, at the turn of the sixth and fourth centuries, imposed itself and consolidated along with the concept of philosophy: the concept of *politics.* The new lemma, as the German historian Christian Meier has shown, is the result of the substantiation of a family of adjectives referring to the *polis*: from *polites* (citizen), to *politikós* (politician), to *Politéia* (Constitution, Ordering of the Polis or, according to the Latin version of the title of Plato's celebrated dialogue, *Res Publica*). The Greeks, 'the Europeans' *par excellence*, are free men precisely in that they live in the *koinonía*, the common space of the Polis and, occupying this space as their *naturally artificial* habitat as linguistic and dialogical animals, they practice *politics*. A sphere that only with Aristotle's work of the same name definitively attains a conceptual status, becoming an expression, along with ethics, of *epistéme praktiké*: of that 'practical science' that does not model conceptual artefacts, like *epistéme theoretiké*, or produce technical and artistic works, like *epistéme poietiké*, but resolves itself into *praxis* – that is, into a specific mode of doing, 'acting' – that has its purpose in itself. Politics, the activity proper to man as *zoon politikón* (as, moreover, philosophy, the activity proper to man as *zoon lógon échon*), can take place only in the space of the polis, outside of which, Aristotle observes, no human can live, but only a beast or a god: 'whoever is unable to enter into an organized community or, because of his self-sufficiency, does not feel the need to do so, is not part of the City (*polis*) and consequently is either a beast (*therion*) or a god' (*Pol.*, I, 1253a, 27–29).

It is worth pointing out here a phenomenon to which we will have to return in the final part of our discussion: the bifurcation between two distinct models of the city that we have inherited from the classical world with the concepts of *polis* and *civitas*. *This* is the phenomenon that Benveniste addressed in an essay that originally appeared in 1970 in a volume in honour of Claude Lévi-Strauss and later collected in the second tome of *Problems of General Linguistics*.[19] Whereas in Greek *polis* is the primary term from which the term *polítes is* derived, in Latin the relationship is diametrically reversed: *civis* is the primary term and *civitas* the derived term. The reason for this seemingly paradoxical inversion is rooted in two different paradigms of 'city': one founded on the priority of the dimension of the *polis* as a *hólon*, a self-founded totality to which the citizen belongs; the other on the idea of *civitas* as a dynamic entity resulting from the relations among *cives*. If in the Greek model of the city one does not give citizens without the holistic presupposition of the polis, in the Latin model one does not give civitas without the relational presupposition of the practices that citizens establish among themselves. While, therefore, the *polites* bears within itself the mark of belonging-dependence on a holistically prefigured *koinonía*, the *civis* is constituted through the cipher of relationship-sharing with the other as *civis meus*, my fellow citizen or compatriot, as distinct from the other as *hostis*, a foreigner in the double sense of guest and enemy.

We shall see later on the decisive implications of this paradigmatic bifurcation of *polis* and *civitas*, destined to mark, far beyond the tradition of 'republicanism', the subsequent vicissitudes of the ideas of the *commons* and *constitutional patriotism*. The node on which we now need to dwell is that relating to the specific features of Greek political holism and the image of order that descends from it. As the proper space of the *human* (a term presumptively universal but actually coinciding with the *Hellenic ethnos*), the polis bears within itself *naturaliter* a grammar of order: therein lies the unbridgeable furrow between the Aristotelian model and the Hobbesian model (the matrix of the different variants of modern contractualism which, though with divergent or antithetical visions of the state of nature, descend from a common individualistic presupposition). But – and the weight of this *but cannot be* stressed enough – the fact that it possesses a grammar does not mean that it possesses a syntax. *Grammar* means that no authentically human life is given except in the common, together natural–artificial and social–political context of the polis. But the *way in which* within the *hólon* and *koinonía* the order of things, relations, and laws should organize itself no longer pertains to the 'generative grammar' of the polis but rather to its *syntax*: that is, to the *Politéia*. The difference between the classical model and the modern contractualist model is thus not reducible to a contrast between full and empty, nature and artifice. As with Hobbes, there is a *problem of order for* Aristotle. Only this problem does not concern the very fact, the grammar, of Order as in Hobbes (for whom human individuals would naturally be asocial and apolitical), but only its form, its syntax. The very *fact of* order, the holistic space of the polis, is certainly not safe from threats or traumatic events: social upheavals or natural events capable of producing a shattering of the *koinon* (think of the description of the plague in Thucydides). But beyond events of that nature, the form of order is subject to that domain of contingency from which the phenomenon of *metabolé politeión* arises: the metabolic cycle of *politiká syntágmata*, of constitutions or 'forms of government'.

It was seen earlier how 'European ideology' rests on a political antithesis situated in perfect parallel with the 'spiritual' West–East dualism: the freedom–despotism antithesis. To this antithesis it could be objected that the classical typology of forms of government, represented by the monarchy–aristocracy–democracy trinomial and their respective degenerations, expressed, in Machiavelli's words, by the triad tyranny–oligarchy–oclocracy (or 'power of the masses', according to Polybius' definition), also contemplates in Greece, in the very cradle of Europe and the West, the tyrannical form of government. However, even with regard to this form of government, the Greek conceptual and symbolic device includes within itself a justification such as to safeguard the tightness of the line of demarcation from Eastern otherness. And the core of justification refers in turn to another antithesis: the legitimacy–illegitimacy antithesis. Tyranny, although a deplorable form of government, being the unrestrained rule of one, is an *illegitimate* form of government insofar as it is exercised over a people of the free: the *demos* of the Europeans, that is, the Greeks. Oriental despotism, on the contrary, is not even a degenerate *polity* (since even this degeneration presupposes the dimension of the polis and, within it, of political action), but a form of rule that is *legitimate insofar* as it is exercised over a mass of non-freedmen. The axiological scope of such an opposition leaves, of course, in the background a number of sociocultural premises of polis civilization, which Aristotle himself tends to 'naturalize': the *demos does* not, as is well known, include all those who inhabit the space of the so-called City-State but only includes free and native adult males capable of accessing the public, properly political and deliberative sphere of the polis. Women and slaves occupy, in fact, the 'subspace' of the *oikos*, relegated to the sphere of that *oikonomía* that serves as a functional productive substructure to materially support the 'life of the polis' and to ensure that members of the *demos are* freed from labour obligations in order to devote themselves entirely to 'politics', that is, the governance of the 'public thing'. Thus, the hidden meaning of *eleutheria is* squared: freedom means, yes, on the one hand, to deliberate together the fate of the 'commune', but, on the other hand and in the first place, to be *free from labour*, from the constraints of economic necessity (it is not for nothing that a certain Karl

Marx, a great admirer of Aristotle, will outline precisely from this model his idea of communism as a passage from the 'realm of necessity' to the 'realm of freedom'). But there is another side, at once parallel and complementary to the *horizontal* demarcation line of the 'democratic' space of the *agora* between men and women, free and slaves: and that is the *vertical* boundary drawn between natives and foreigners. By 'foreigners' one must mean not only 'barbarians', individuals from other linguistic-cultural backgrounds, but also Greeks originating from other *poleis*. The Stranger of Elea, to evoke a *topos* from the Platonic dialogues, could certainly, as a Greek, be welcomed and be heard in Athens in a context of common discourse, but he could never attain Athenian citizenship. Work conducted by ancient historians in recent decades has shown that one of the main causes of the decline of the great civilization of the polis is to be found in the inexorable entropic tendency induced by the 'myth of autochthony': by the interdict to contemplate the opening of citizenship to foreigners. On this aspect, too, as we shall see at the end, the contrastive comparison between the model-polis and the model-civitas is bound to play a decisive function. But let us see, meanwhile, to project the implications of these distant assumptions onto the constellation of our present.

Double Movement

The original scenes from which we took our cue continue to be influential even today, despite the fact that today's *theatrum globi*, unlike the seventeenth-century *theatrum mundi*, no longer has Europe as a protagonist. As Carl Schmitt had captured in that extraordinary foreshadowing of the new planetary arrangements represented by *The Nomos of the Earth*, the leading actor on the global stage is the American West, which, *against Europe*, stands as the subject of adventure, of the frontier, of productivity, of technological innovation, of the fulfilment of a 'space revolution' hinging on the shift from land to sea to air – and, therefore, as the legitimate guarantor of Liberty. Care must be taken, however. The Schmittian diagnosis hits the mark, exhibiting undoubted descriptive relevance, only in relation to the Cold War phase. Projecting it *sic et simpliciter* onto today risks producing misleading effects, to say the least. After the end of the bipolar system, the *Worldpicture* is radically changed. It is, however, a change that is as radical as it is paradoxical: since the collapse of the Soviet Empire, instead of resolving itself into a 'Westernization of the world' (as Serge Latouche has argued polemically and Francis Fukuyama apologetically), has given rise to a *double movement* of standardization and differentiation, spatial compression, and temporal diaspora. Moreover, with good grace to Schmitt, even in the new proscenium Europe and the West remain not only inextricably united in roots but above all involved in the same destiny. Those who, oblivious or oblivious to the lessons of the great nineteenth- to twentieth-century European culture from Tocqueville to Weber, turn the Europe–America tension into an oppositional pair only reproduce the old adage of the 'Konservative Revolution': according to which Europe should distinguish itself from the West by rediscovering the roots of its own *Kultur*, devitalized by the entropic process of *Zivilisation*. Faced with the re-proposal, sometimes from a reversed ideological side, of similar theses, we must remember that Europe is, from its origins, a culture of civilization, technique, and navigation. Technique originated essentially as a technique for the government of navigation: and, as we know, the most sophisticated technical equipment is needed primarily at sea, not on land. Thus, technique is not Ernst Jünger's machinic apparatus, nor is it Heidegger's *Gestell*: much closer to a frame or an implant than to a 'post-Fordist' technological device. Technique is precisely the function of a culture that understands itself as a traveling civilization: a civilization that constantly moves the frontier line forward, moving from a virtually perspectival view of space, destined to project outward. Therein lies the at once 'ratioid' (never has the neologism coined by Robert Musil in antithesis to 'rational' been as valid as it is today) and 'visionary' attitude of the West, which will find full expression with the invention of Renaissance perspective.

But here we must also look for the distant premise of the 'global', which, from the symbolic point of view, coincides with the genesis of 'enlightenment', in the sense in which Adorno and Horkheimer speak of it in the *Dialectic of the Enlightenment*. This is not, of course, about the Enlightenment as a historical period or as a movement of thought, but about the *Aufklärung*, the razioid enlightenment typical of the West. The influential scene of the first enlightenment, of the original enlightenment, is – as is well known, but always useful to remember – the figure of Odysseus. 'Rational' enlightenment and world navigation coincide. The global, from this point of view, is not a recent event but is innervated in the symbolic structure of the West since its origins. For these assumptions to be historically translated into actual hegemony, however, one must wait for the advent of the modern age. The earlier experiences of Alexander's Empire and the Roman Empire, despite the exceptional duration of the latter, were unable to reverse, as Arnold Toynbee pointed out at the time, the relationship between the World and the West, between 'the World and the West' into a relationship between 'The West and the Rest', between the West and the Rest of the World. In some respects, indeed, the earlier imperial dominions were not processes of 'Westernization of the World' at all, but rather were situated in a field of tension between East and West (or, in the case of the Alexandrian empire, even gave rise on the cultural level to an 'Orientalization of the World'). The *turning point* at which the inversion of relations between the world and the West takes place is thus to be found in the economic-technological take-off that, between the fourteenth and sixteenth centuries, will enable a small region of the planet, Europe, to progressively extend – thanks to the combination of 'sails and cannons', Carlo Cipolla's deadly pair – their hegemony over the rest of the world. Hence was born the globalization that serves as a preamble and prerequisite to what has been called the *Neuzeit*, the New Age. In its operational acquisition, then, the global is at one with the genesis of modernity. Modernity is therefore unthinkable without the opening of the seas, without the design-productive 'representation' of the Earth as a circumnavigable sphere that serves as the premise for the conquest of the New World. On the subject, I discovered significant points of convergence between my philosophical approach to the topic of globalization and the way in which Peter Sloterdijk – in his three-volume *opus Sphären* – took up, in contrast to the German ideology of continental-terranean rootedness, the Nietzschean motif of navigation as *Erfahrung*, and journey of experience.[20] Modernity was born when the Earth finally became a sphere, not only geometrically but also technically and operationally: the circumnavigation of the globe takes the original idea of navigation as an adventure to the extreme, which finds emblematic expression in the Hanseatic motto *Navigare necesse est, vivere non necesse*. Without navigation there is no life. A life without navigation, like a sedentary existence that renounces *curiositas* understood as the journey of experience, amounts to a non-life. Therefore, navigation, like any authentic experience, is a prize unto itself. Not *in spite of*, but *because of* the shipwreck: *Naufragium feci, bene navigavi*. We now better understand why postmodern theses do not fully grasp the problem of our time: the phenomenon of deterritorialization is a process inherent in modernity, not a characteristic feature of postmodernity. Modernity coincides with the breaking out into the open of the West's original vocation, with the cross-border and 'uprooting' thrust of the bourgeois revolution, admirably summarized, in the *Manifesto* of Marx and Engels, by the phrase *Alles Ständische und Stehende verdampft*: everything solid vanishes into the air, everything substantial evaporates. ... Yet.

Yet that same Modernity that was born under the banner of cosmopolitan globalism and the rupture of communitarian and cetual-corporative enclosures is the era in which the most entrenched and cohesive form of domination that has ever appeared in human history was established: the territorially closed sovereign nation state. How do we explain the coexistence in capitalist modernity between the cross-border and deterritorializing vocation and the domination of a quintessentially territorial and bounded by rigid borders form like the state? This is precisely where Giovanni Arrighi comes to our aid with his thesis of a Modern marked by the co-presence of two principles: the 'principle of worldliness' and the 'principle of territoriality'. The field of tension constituted by the two principles can give rise, depending on the case, to cyclical alternation (with the periodic prevalence of one or the other) or to conflicting cohabitation (within the same phase of the cycle). But the opposing injunctions they determine provide us with the paradoxical figure of the ancipitous nature, or *dual soul*, of capitalist modernity: at once state and anti-state. The Janus face of modern capitalist power, with the bipolar oscillation that characterizes it between rootedness and uprootedness, territoriality and extra-territoriality, is a constant that has spanned, from the sixteenth to the nineteenth centuries, the four 'long centuries' of modernity and that the 'long 20th century' (Arrighi again) has reproduced and taken to the extreme.

'Oikonomía' and 'Politéia': Robinson's World and the Birth of Political Economy

In recent decades it has become a mantra of international philosophical discussion to emphasize the centrality, for the modern, of the theological–political element: through Carl Schmitt and Walter Benjamin, the discourse on sovereignty has ended up revolving once again around the relations between decision and norm, legitimacy and legality, placing the previously mentioned theme of the 'state of exception' at the centre. No one could greet this *revival* with greater satisfaction than the author of these pages: having been the first in Italy to devote a university course after the Second World War to Schmitt's 'concept of the political' at the University of Naples 'L'Orientale' (academic year 1977–1978) and to take up its themes in relation to European Marxism in a book that appeared soon after.[21] It should be added, however, that the sovereignty-state nexus of exception concerns only one part, not all of modernity. There is another half of the modern narrative whose genealogy is not linearly traceable to political theology: it is that embryo of the modern governmental *ratio brought into* focus by Foucault and genealogically retraced along the tracks of an 'economic theology' by the works of Gerhard Richter and Giorgio Agamben. However, the illuminating Foucauldian dissociation of *government* and *sovereignty* could be contrasted with the detection of the presence, at the heart of the first properly modern foundation of sovereign power (which is due to Hobbes not, as postulated *pro domo sua* by Schmitt, to a Bodin read in a decisionist key from the definition of sovereignty as 'absolute power to create and abrogate law'), of a theological-economic motif discernible in an idea of calculistic *ratio* hinged ultimately on a secularized version of the theological casuistry of the lesser evil. *Homo æqualis* (let us not forget that Hobbes is a radical theorist of equality, who already in *De Cive* transcends the multi-millennial fence between men and women) makes his entry into modernity *alone*. Threatened by nature and his fellows the individual leads a *nasty, brutish and short* life but, like a pirate seeking free spaces on the seas, he is animated by an inexhaustible desire for power, wealth, and glory that leads him to conflate with other individuals, driven by the same infinity of desire, in a war that tends to be deadly. Animated as he is by self-asserting passions, only the extreme passion, fear, is able to arouse in him the faculty of *ratio*, the conjecture that, through cost–benefit calculation, leads him to opt for the only possible way out: to agree with others on common submission to a Power capable of guaranteeing the life of each and all. Let us pay attention to the most crucial and problematic sequence of Hobbesian reasoning. The drive exerted by the passions is matched in human nature by the *recta ratio* of interest and calculation. This is why modern individualism can only be understood by integrating the theological–political perspective with the theological–economic perspective. The telltale of the problem can be seen in the very word by which, beginning with Hobbes, the constitutive covenant of the political order is named: *covenant*, a term from Old French (introduced into England with the Norman invasion of 1066) that stands for 'convention', 'agreement', and 'contract' understood as 'transaction'. As if the sovereignty of the great Leviathan, the effect of the *pactum subjectionis*, flows from a consensual agreement, or *pactum unionis*, between individuals who, paradoxically, agree on the basis of an institution of private law, not public law. There is no public dimension, no 'social bond' or 'People', prior to the creation of the artifice of sovereignty. The King–People dualism, with the 'dim sovereignty' that characterizes it, pre-exists only in the scenarios of medieval political theology, in the terms of a bilateral agreement between the Christian Prince and the People, designed to guarantee mutual observance of the norms of natural law: with the possibility for the People to rebel against an unjust monarch and for the latter to repress a seditious people. In Hobbes (and in modern contractualism in general) the suppression of this 'pre-existence' involves both terms of the pair. Whereas in medieval political theology subjects precede the contract, in the Hobbesian model they are constituted by the contract itself. There is no People before the institution *via* contract of Sovereign Power: hence, the subject that gives rise to the *pactum unionis* is not yet People but *multitude of* individuals. A collection of independent wills that, by uniting, perform the first 'corporate' act, *suspending* the *ius in omnia* into which jusnaturalism has plummeted (after the collapse of the teleological vision induced by the new Galilean world-image) and *interrupting* the endemic conflictual seriality of the state of nature. The result of the second act, the *pactum subjectionis*, will no longer have the form of a bilateral contract but that of a *contract in favour of a third party*: of a 'third actor' to whom the individuals gathered in the multitude decide to alienate all their rights in nature (all but one: the right to *conservatio vitae*). Only once the sovereign Person is established – whose artificial character in many respects represents a development of the medieval Jungianist notion of *persona* ficta – and the positive law produced by it, can the multitude of equal and different individuals finally represent itself as the People: not a cultural or sociological entity (as Hans Kelsen had well captured in his polemic with Carl Schmitt), but a legal subject brought into being by the sovereign power of Leviathan.

Thus the two sides of the Hobbesian paradox emerge:

(a) the absoluteness of Sovereign Power (not to be confused with any form of totalitarianism, in the sense given to this term by Hannah Arendt: the rule of Leviathan – as Carl Schmitt and Reinhart Koselleck have well argued in this regard – stops at the threshold of the 'inner forum' of consciousness, does not claim inner adherence but only external obedience to its positive laws) is the 'lesser evil' in the face of the need to get out of an extreme condition represented by the mortal threat inherent in the 'generative grammar' of conflict proper to the state of nature;

(b) although the influential scene of the *bellum omnium contra omnes* is not represented, as Crawford Brough Macpherson had assumed in his 1962 work on the 'political theory of possessive individualism', by the competitive capitalist market, but rather, according to Norberto Bobbio's indication, by civil war: the exit from the state of nature leverages in Hobbes an individualistic *rationale*, hinged on cost–benefit calculus, which bears in embryo the characteristic features of the economic paradigm of 'rational choice'. For a full unfolding of this paradigm, we must wait for a crucial event, destined to deeply mark the development of knowledge and forms of organization in Western society. This event coincides with the birth of a new science called *political economy*: associating, in a kind of oxymoron, the two dimensions of *polis* and *oikos*, which classical civilization had kept distinct and hierarchically compartmentalized. From then on, the 'wealth of nations' would become, in the West, the main factor in the legitimization of power, and the fate of politics could no longer be separated from the practices of governing the economy and controlling the population.

The interpenetration between *oikonomía* and *politéia* has deeply reshaped the sociocultural and symbolic arrangements of the Order in the transition from 'modern space' to 'global space'. But here it is necessary not to lose sight of the internal complexity of a dynamic of change involving both moments: a dynamic that cannot be simplified in the terms of a transit from modern to postmodern. Both modern and global space give rise to complex configurations and dissonant *field effects*. As early as the Modern, the dimension of Euclidean spatiality (the reference point of the metaphysical–political systems of Descartes, Hobbes, and Spinoza) presents a crack produced by the bifurcation of the West into two models of order:

(a) the *continental model* centred on the concept of sovereignty and the trinomial State–Population–Territory;

(b) the *oceanic model*, hinged on the concept of *government* and the image of the political order as a *community of communities* and a network of associations.

To the former model seems to correspond the compact and continuous image of the pyramid, and to the latter the polycentric and discontinuous image of the archipelago. Thus, on the one hand we have the predominance of the terrestrial element, of the symbolism of the 'mainland', in which the boundaries are always sharply and unequivocally fixed; on the other hand, we have the predominance of the maritime element, of the symbolism of navigation and the frontier. In this way, a dualism between two legal models was generated: on the one hand, the *civil law* model, characterized by the prevalence of legal systematics; on the other hand, the *common law* model, based predominantly not on the code, not on dogmatics but on casuistry, not on legislation but on practice, custom and jurisdiction (the famous jurisprudence of the Courts).

But at this point the question inevitably arises: What is the relationship of continuity/discontinuity between modern space and global space?

Global Space: Uniformity and Diaspora

Compared with modern spatiality, global space, marked by the transition from modernity-nation to modernity-world, exhibits a non-Euclidean configuration, irreducible to a homogeneous map. The post-Hobbesian order (or disorder) of *glo-calization* is not readable in the light of a mono-logic, albeit functionally or systemically differentiated, but appears, on the contrary, to be dominated by an alienating bi-logic, marked by the co-presence of techno-economic standardization and diaspora of world-regions, communities, and life forms whose behaviours escape the economic paradigm of *rational choice*. The two sides of mercantile, financial and technological-communicative homogenization and cultural-identity differentiation, however, do not oppose each other in a static alternative but interpenetrate dynamically, giving rise to the phenomenon of *global production of locality*. The local is no longer territorial, in the sense of Euclidean spatiality, it is not a section or subsystem of the global, but its *fold*: the inevitable and elusive implication of the Realm of Quantity imposed by communicative-mercantile codification. Inside the fold, movements enacted by 'diasporic communities' sometimes produce thresholds of resistance and counteroffensive marked by an identity obsession close to fundamentalism. But the very phenomenon of so-called fundamentalism (or rather: of fundamentalisms) is not a legacy of the past or tradition (which fundamentalisms punctually invent or reinvent) but – as Shmuel N. Eisenstadt has documented – a modern event. A phenomenon, we add, that becomes proliferating in global hypermodernity because of the perverse mechanism of removal-reification generated by the dual logic that governs it: globalization, *this* digital-communicative-financial globalization, *by removing* the symbolic-identity dimension with the claim of its absorption into the spectacular imagery of the planetary Emporium, triggers the backlash, compensatory and retaliatory, of the reified identities with which not only diasporic communities but the great postcolonial civilizations themselves are self-represented (think of the contrast between *Asian values* and *Western values*). Thus emerges the latent mechanics of global bilogics: globalization, instead of universalizing, as its apologists continue to claim, *de-universalizes* and, in spite of the exponential growth of *métissage*, makes the forms of life of civilizations and human communities idiosyncratic. Within this game of mirrors, the fundamentalist drift of 'differences' replicates, with its identity obsession, the logic of identity that has shaped the world-system.

To rethink the universal in the age of globalization means, therefore, first and foremost to *break the* mirror: to go beyond the specular antithesis between universalism of identity (Enlightenment-style) and anti-universalism of difference (relativist-style), through the proposal (advanced by me in *Passage to the West*) of a *universalism of difference.* The adoption of such a formula moves from a twofold theoretical requirement: (a) to understand *difference* not as a place or a subject, but as an optical vertex, a *criterion* for the construction of the universal; (b) to assume the universal as an *unsaturated formula*, starting from a theorem of incompleteness, avoiding falling back into the old-new adage of Western supremacism, whereby (constant of the enlightened versions, *à la* Kant, or trivial, Fukuyama style) the House of the Universal, designed by the Enlightenment of Reason and put in place by the Rationality of the Market, would now be ready to welcome the whole world into its Civilization of law, competition and free democratic competition. Instead, to move from the assumption of incompleteness is to remember, with Raimon Panikkar, that the House of the Universal is not already built but must be multilaterally constructed and reconstructed, thanks to the universalizing thrusts coming from the planet's great cultures and multiple communities and forms of life (human and non-human).

The grounds of difference as a criterion and of the universal as a 'horizon in motion', tabulated at multiple entrances susceptible to reception of the most diverse and unexpected universalizing thrusts, call into play what we might call the 'secular arm' of universalism of difference: the program of an escape from the aporias of the two main models of inclusion in the sphere of citizenship theorized and practised so far by the modern West. I refer to the republican assimilationist model and the strong multiculturalist or 'mosaic' model. Again, the aporias presented by the two models appear to be opposite and mirror each other: if the former, which we might call the *model-République*, functions as a system of indifference in which citizenship absorbs and neutralizes all ethno-cultural, religious, and sexual differences (after affirming the latter in its *Declaration of the Rights of Women and Citizens*, Olympe de Gouges was guillotined), the second, provocatively definable as the *model-Londonistan*, contemplates the sphere of citizenship as a system of contiguous ghettos, of armored differences, arranged next to each other in the manner of incommunicating islands or monads without doors or windows. The rupture of this perverse *Spiegelspiel* between homogenizing undifferentiation and static representation of 'differences' requires the *transcendence of the identity logic that unites them*. Such a transcendence cannot merely follow the edifying path of procedural agreement (in the sense of John Rawls' *overlapping consensus*), mutual recognition, or dialogic-communicative understanding (according to Jürgen Habermas' proposal) but rather must give rise to a confrontation between different experiences and narratives aimed at bringing out the ideas of the universal that each difference has come to accrue autonomously. This should be, in the global era, the task of what is emphatically called the 'democratic public sphere'. In the perspective opened up by the universalism of difference, democracy must be radically redefined as a synthesis of *politics-process* (in Hannah Arendt's sense) and *politics-event* (in Machiavelli's kairological sense) that can no longer be framed in the classical and modern typology of forms of government.

But there is another node in the global scene with which such a program is called to contend. It is only today that experts in international politics seem to have noticed the ancipite logic of globalization: of the conflicting cohabitation of uniformity and diaspora that punctuates its times and reshapes its spatial configurations. Behind the babelic façade of the world turned globe (represented, better than by any sociological synthesis, by Alejandro Gonzáles Inárritu's film *Babel*), a specific dynamic spring from the intertwining of planetary homogenization and fragmentation: the return of a politics of the great spaces mediated, unlike in the 1930s, by strategies that are no longer and not only geopolitical but rather geoeconomic and geocultural. The emergence of the Brics (Brazil, Russia, India, China, and South Africa), with their hybrid forms of economy, stands to signal two aspects likely to shape our future. First, the global scenario of our present is perhaps another exciting chapter in the 'great transformation' Karl Polanyi spoke of. Second, the coming to prominence of new protagonists with historical and anthropological-cultural backgrounds significantly or radically different from that of the West stands to show that global capital, despite the immense deployment of financial power and the universal display of commodity-form images and logos, is capable, yes, of giving rise to a global market, but not of producing a global society. When confronted with different civilizational contexts, global capital finds itself forced, like a chameleon, to adapt to pre-existing ethical foundations and sociocultural forms, thus resulting in hybrid and in many ways unprecedented forms of capitalism. This is particularly evident in the case of China, whose 'capital-communism' belies the Western equation between capitalism and individualistic ethics, basing development and productivity on hierarchical-communal associational structures and the subordination of individual goals (and, of course, rights) to those of collective entities (family, firm, group, and state). To the pincer constituted by the two opposing models of globalization – the individualistic-competitive model of the 'American' colossus (the United States *in primis*) and the paternalistic-communitarian model of the 'Asian' colossus (China *in primis*) – Europe is called upon to provide its own autonomous response, an alternative model that can neither be squeezed on either horn of the dilemma, nor resolve itself into a compromising mediation. Of vital elements of this *Tertium*, not to be confused with yet another 'third way' (of third ways, we know, are paved the European cemeteries of the twentieth century), Europe already has in the rich cultural baggage of its history: in the idea of an individual who is not isolated and competitive but relational and supportive (*No man is an Island*, wrote John Donne, way back in 1634, in *Meditation XVII* of the *Devotions upon emergent Occasions*) and in the idea of a community that is neither organic and terran nor hierarchical-authoritarian but marked by the criterion of difference and the valorization of the irreducible uniqueness and singularity of each person.

A Europe less captive to financial and technobureaucratic constraints and capable of translating this potential of thought and culture into politics could play a valuable function today in the non-Euclidean, at once interdependent and polycentric space of the globalized world. By enhancing the novelty of its multilevel institutional arrangement, which is unmatched in any of the political forms known to date, the European Union could also point other countries to the prospect of a global Constitutionalism in which political processes are delineated less and less in terms of sovereignty and more and more in terms of dynamic balance and mutual limitation among a plurality of instances.

But what then is the *parádeigma*, the functional model for the pursuit of such an objective? The idea of overcoming the vertical logic of sovereignty in favour of a horizontal arrangement of what a great Italian jurist such as Massimo Severo Giannini, in a provocatively anti-Hobbesian formula, called the different and autonomous 'sovereign powers', presents itself very close to the Machiavellian model, for which optimal is that republic in which 'one power looks at the other': and it goes without saying that this is a look that is by no means contemplative. The reference to Machiavelli directly calls into question the concept of *civitas*, understood – in the wake of the decisive contributions of Étienne Balibar and Pietro Costa – as a reference to an enlarged and post-state idea of citizenship, understood as a political–legal space that is not identifiably pre-constituted but *incremental*: a *civitas augescens* susceptible to accommodate within itself a plurality of different *nationes*, *gentes*, cultures, and religious confessions.

The syntagma *civitas augescens* refers to a key concept in the Roman legal tradition, documented over the centuries by the work of various authors: from Ennius (*Ann.*, 478) to Cicero (*Pro Balbo*, 13.31), from Sallust (*De Catilinae coniur.*, 6.7, 7.3, 10.1) to Livy (4.4.4, 8.13.16). The idea behind it – the growth of the People and the enlargement of citizenship – runs through the history of Rome from its origins, finding its topical moment in the *Constitutio Antoniniana* and its landing point in Justinian, with the elimination of the category of 'foreigner'. To take on this dynamic, incremental, and 'inclusive' vision (without silencing the constitutive ambivalence of the term) as the symbolic and cultural-conceptual background of the challenges facing Europe in our global present is not to adumbrate solutions in a dualistic key (such as Mediterranean Europe vs. Northern Europe or 'Latin Empire' vs. 'Central European Reich'), but rather to pick up the broken thread of the discourse around citizenship in a time marked by the progressive decline of the modern state-form: of an image of political community hinged on the towering notion of sovereignty and the identity paradigm of *reductio ad Unum*.

In the face of global challenges, the notion of *civitas* thus appears more adequate than the classical notion of *polis* and the modern notion of *nation state* to come to grips with the unresolved contradiction of modern democracy: that between the 'universalist vocation' of principles and the selectivity of the devices that sanction and regulate membership in the political community. Along this track, it is possible to pose a twofold need: the need for a *democratic politics of translation* hinged on an 'anthropology of citizenship' and the prospect of a universalism of difference, sharply demarcated from both Enlightenment-derived identity universalism (republican assimilationist model) and differentialist anti-universalism ('strong' multiculturalist model, structured as a mosaic of contiguous ghettos, of noncommunicating islands).

Never before have objective conditions been so propitious for a crucial role of Europe, of the European *Tertium*, on the stage of the globalized world. Never before have the subjective conditions of European politicians and ruling groups appeared so inadequate for the task and incapable of grasping the signs of the times. And yet.

And yet, to conclude again with a classic quote, taken not coincidentally from the most famous Latin text on wrath: *In omni servitute apertam libertati viam.*[22]

Notes

1 Cf. G. Marramao, *Potere e secolarizzazione*, Bollati Boringhieri, Turin 2005 (new and expanded edition).
2 Cf. C. Schmitt, *Nomos-Nahme-Name*, in *Der Beständige Aufbruch. Festschrift für Erich Przywara*, ed. by Siegfried Behn, Verlag Glock und Lutz, Nürnberg 1959, pp. 92–105.
3 Cf. G. Semerano, *Le origini della cultura europea*, II, Olschki Florence 1994, pp. 545–546; Id., *L'infinito: un equivoco millenario. Le antiche civiltà del Vicino Oriente e le origini del pensiero greco* (The Ancient Near Eastern Civilizations and the Origins of Greek Thought), Bruno Mondadori, Milan 2001, p. 249.
4 Ibid, p. 248.
5 É. Benveniste, *Le Vocabulaire des institutions indo-européennes*, II: *Pouvoir, droit, religion*, Éditions de Minuit, Paris 1969; transl.it., *Il vocabolario delle istituzioni indoeuropee*, II: *Potere, diritto, religione*, Einaudi, Turin 1976, p. 294.
6 Ibid., pp. 294–295.
7 Ibid., p. 397.
8 L. Muraro, *Authority*, Rosenberg & Sellier, Turin 2013, p. 59.
9 The reading of the current global Babel as a suspended time or 'interregnum' between a no-more and a not-yet was already proposed by me in the first italian edition (2003) of *The Passage the West*, Verso, London-New York 2012 and in *La passione del presente*, Bollati Boringhieri, Turin 2008, in terms in some respects similar to those later envisaged by the book-dialogue by Zygmunt Bauman and Ezio Mauro, *Babel*, Laterza, Roma-Bari 2015.
10 Cf. E. Fornari, *Boundary Lines: Philosophy and postcolonialism*, SUNY Press, New York 2020.
11 Cf. G. Marramao, The *Passage West*, cit.

12   K. Jaspers, *Vom Ursprung und Ziel der Geschichte*, Piper, München 1949; transl.it., *Origine e senso della storia*, Edizioni di Comunità, Milan 1972, p. 95.

13   Ibid., p. 96.

14   Ibid., p. 98.

15   I echo here a number of remarks made in *Passage to the West*, cit. pp. 19ff.; 67ff.

16   M. Weber, *Gesammelte Aufsätze zur Religionssoziologie*, J.C.B. Mohr, Tübingen 1920–21, I, p. 1; transl.it., *Sociology of Religion*, Community, Milan 2002, I, p. 5.

17   J. Bottéro, *Mésopotamie: l'écriture, la raison et les dieux*, Gallimard, Paris 1987; transl.it., *Mesopotamia. Writing, Mentality and the Gods*, Einaudi, Turin 1991.

18   M. Bernal, *Black Athena: Afro-Asiatic Roots of Classical Civilization*, 3 vols. (1987–2006); transl.it., *Black Athena. Afro-Asiatic Roots of Classical Civilization*, Il Saggiatore, Milan 2011.

19   Cf. É. Benveniste, *Problèmes de linguistique général II*, Gallimard, Paris 1974: transl.it., *Problemi di linguistica generale II*, Il Saggiatore, Milan 1985, pp. 272–280.

20   Cf. P. Sloterdijk, *Sphären I – Blasen, Mikrosphärologie*, Suhrkamp, Frankfurt am Main 1998; *Sphären II - Globen, Makrosphärologie*, ibid. 1999; *Sphären III – Schäume, Plurale Sphärologie*, ibid. 2004.

21   G. Marramao, *Il Politico e le trasformazioni*, De Donato, Bari 1979; updated and expanded English edition, *The Bewitched World of Capital: Economic Crisis and the Metamorphosis of the Political*, Brill, Leiden-Boston 2023.

22   Seneca, *De Ira*, III, xv. ["In any state of servitude the way to freedom is open."]

6 Epilogue

The New World Scene

No Sovereign, No Indisputable Power

Give me the map there, commands King Lear in the opening scene of Shakespeare's tragedy.

But meanwhile, the map of power has changed in the new structure of the world, and there is no Sovereign, no indisputable Power capable of distributing it. We see it strikingly with the return of war to the heart of the European continent. The 'winds of war' materialized in a dramatic event that, in violation of international law, sees the return of a war conflict in the heart of Europe: with devastation, deaths of men, women, and children, thousands of refugees forced to leave their homes and take refuge in other countries of the continent (from Poland to Germany, passing through Italy).

An authentic humanitarian catastrophe, for which Putin's expansionist strategy is undoubtedly responsible, which seeks to not only annex but literally swallow all the territories that previously belonged to the Soviet Union, in a neo-Tsarist imperial project that even seems to refer to the Russia of Peter the Great.

At the same time, however, we cannot hide the political responsibilities of the United States and Europe in promoting Ukraine's NATO membership: How much wiser would the proposal for that country to join the European Union have been? This confirms the new world scenario that I had outlined in some of my works: a new multipolarism no longer hegemonized by nation states but by continent-states, whose objectives seem to confirm the risk of a fragmented Third World War, of the that he had recently spoken to Pope Francis.

But we had already seen evidence of the new logic, of the new system of world powers, with the clashes in the G20 and Cop26 on the management of the pandemic and the point of no return on climate change. There is only one way to understand the reasons: to take note of the uselessness of the old maps of the State, the economy, and society, building new maps capable of guiding us in the apparently indecipherable logic that presides over the game of alliances and conflicts, disrupting the traditional hierarchies of influence between the different actors on the planetary scene: political elites, financial powers, and movements.

DOI: 10.4324/9781032632827-6

No Map: The Non-Euclidean Spatiality of the World

A scenario, in many ways unprecedented, of a world that is anything but 'liquid', shaped by the non-Euclidean spatiality of a global dynamic in which uniformity induces diaspora, interdependence generates divisive effects, and techno-economic deterritorialization turns into political (or even war) reterritorialization. It is then inevitable that anyone who thought of globalization in 'Euclidean' terms, as a linear process destined to spread homogeneously over a smooth surface, would find themselves proclaiming (sadly or triumphantly) its end. In reality, the nature of this globalization (in many aspects different from the previous ones that have marked the course of history) is precisely that of presenting itself with an ancipite profile, with a double logic. The 'time–space compression' (David Harvey) between the profoundly different cultures of all the continents has disturbed the relations between East and West, setting in motion an ambivalent process of economic-technological appropriation and identity reaction that, in civilizations with a thousand-year history, such as China, India, and Russia, has given rise to intertwinings between the capitalist market and political power radically different from the historical form of Western societies.

Thus has emerged the phenomenon of continent-states declining 'capitalism' in specific geocultural forms. The domination of global capital – as we have already seen previously and as I highlighted in my book *Dopo il Leviatano* ('After the Leviathan') – does not give rise to a single form of 'capitalism' (a term, moreover, absent from Marx's lexicon and scientifically 'unclouded' only since Werner Sombart and Max Weber), but to a plurality of 'capitalisms' rooted in strongly differentiated ethical-cultural environments in Europe and North America.

Marx: Capital – not Capitalism

Marx would therefore, according to the opinion of some economists and sociologists, be both right and wrong:

right: for having foreseen the expansive dynamics of global capital;
wrong: for having believed that this expansion would automatically lead to a universal homogenization of the world.

But such a judgement does not consider the important rethinking of the late Marx on the future of the capitalist mode of production in civilizational contexts other than Europe and the United States: a rethinking witnessed above all by the *Ethnological Notebooks*.

Thus it happens that the current world map is increasingly marked by the power of 'political capitalisms' represented no longer by nation states, but by continent-states willing to compete with the West and, in the case of China, to confront the United States as the hegemonic power of the global world. We find ourselves, at this point, before a paradox. The exponential growth of sovereignty in countries like China, Russia, and India has as a counterpart in Europe a progressive dispersion of sovereignty: a phenomenon that must be gone to the character of the 'post-national constellation' of the EU (according to the famous expression of Jürgen Habermas) and destined to feed populist and sovereign drives (as in the case of Hungary and some other EU States).

It is difficult to say now if and to what extent the dispersion of sovereignty can be a factor of weakness or, paradoxically, a factor of strength in the face of the centripetal and sovereignist authoritarianism of countries like Russia and China. In any case, those who speak ignorantly of the end of globalization should be reminded that war is only the other side of a global world. A world that is now multipolar: articulated no longer in nation states, as the pathetic European sovereignists think, but in paternalistic-authoritarian continent-states. The only hope is that they push the West to practice democracy and human rights in a less hypocritical and supremacist way than before.

One thing, however, seems certain: only the transition towards a political Europe, towards a sovereign Europe capable of playing the role of global actor, can open the perspective of a democratic alternative, a *tertium*, between neoliberal anarchy and hegemonic temptations and totalitarian.

A *Tertium*, not a 'third way'.

Because of third ways (right or left) the European cemeteries of the twentieth century are paved.

As can be seen in the new image of the world that we have begun to outline, it is an arduous task to try to retain the heart of the present: locate the logic and the structure in it – beyond the noise of the present – to bring them to the concept. It has always been arduous: it was also arduous in the time of Hegel and Marx, and in the time of Weber and Lenin. But today it is even more so: in the present of our 'finite world', spatially compressed and temporally accelerated, and yet increasingly impossible to lead towards a mono-logic. A world that, in reality, seems dominated by the distracting effects of a logic, by virtue of which the standardizing structure of the techno-economy and the global Emporium corresponds to a growing diaspora of identities, values, and life forms.

Between Babel and Kakania

Often in the past I have resorted, due to the discretion of this 'state of the art', to suggestive metaphors taken from literature, such as Musil's Kakania: Isn't our world perhaps a globalization of Kakania? Or collected from 'influential scenes' (in the sense of the Freudian Ur-szene) that go back to the mythical-religious heritage of our civilization, as in the case of Babel: Is not our uniformed world more and more similar, perhaps like the tower of Babel, to a cacophonous compendium of multiple and untranslatable languages?

Ignoring George Steiner's wonderful collection of essays 'After Babel', which goes back as far as 1975, perhaps it is nonetheless difficult today to find a literary text or essay capable of accounting for the captivating bi-logic of Global Babel, with the same intensity and symbolic efficacy of some films or, rather, cinematographic texts. Films are also texts – that is to say, according to the incomparable class of Roland Barthes, woven – which, due to expressive dignity and richness of thought stimuli, have very little to envy to written texts. *Babel* is the title of a suggestive film by Mexican director Alejandro González Iñarritu. In it, the globalized world is described as a babelic space, composed in the form of mosaics of a multiplicity of dispersed pictures of life – at the same time materially unequal and culturally differentiated – linked by fluxes of events that cross them. Macro events, such as the great financial crises, or microscopic events, as in the case of the event from which the film begins: a wandering projectile that, fired by a super-technological rifle used inexpertly by a boy who has stolen it from his father, shepherd in the mountains of Morocco, accidentally ends up against a tour bus, critically injuring a young American (Cate Blanchett) traveling with her husband (Brad Pitt). The effects of the event are unleashed, according to the physical mechanism of the chain reaction, in different contexts of the world, made interdependent by the explosive punctuality of what happened: from Morocco, a still archaic country, to opulent California, where the couple of tourists resides; from the mixture of modernity and tradition of the Mexican people (from where the nanny of the couple's children comes from) to the existential and intergenerational problems of youth communities in the metropolitan condition of contemporary Tokyo (where the Japanese global hunter lives – that just before returning to Japan he had given the rifle to the Moroccan shepherd). It is difficult to deny that the suggestive charge of the film depends on its paradoxical descriptive relevance: from the efficiency with which it illustrates the enigmatic interdependence of a glocalized world, in which differentiation proceeds at the same rate as unification and centrifugal thrusts, autonomist and idiosyncratic are intertwined in an inextricable plexus with the technological-mercantile homologation of lifestyles and consumption. And yet, there is something essential that seems to be missing from this relevant and perspicuous snapshot of our global age. The true stake in the dramatic phase of transition that we are experiencing between modernity-nation and modernity-world, from the no-more of the old interstate order under the hegemony of the West to the not-yet of a new supranational order to be built from In a multilateral way, it cannot be reduced to the alternative between liberalism and communitarianism – or rather: between liberal individualism and communitarianism – nor can it be resolved in a kind of compromise or synthesis between the instances of distributive universalism and identity differentialism.

As Seyla Benhabib opportunely observed in her works, it is now opportune not only to undo the false dilemma between universalism and relativism but also to resolve the impasse of a normative political philosophy that tends to objectify 'cultural identities' and 'struggles for the recognition', assuming these in cal data quality and not as problems.

However, overcoming such stagnant situations (same ones that strongly jeopardize the effectiveness of liberal contractualist theories and John Rawls' own overlapping consensus proposal) is only possible under two conditions.

Firstly, breaking the equation between culture and identity; second, subtract the universal – despite its etymology – from the logic of uniformity and reductio ad Unum, to ascribe it to the regime of multiple and difference.

The foregoing would be equivalent, in other words, to 'breaking the mirror', breaking the specular relationships that we usually establish between 'us' and 'others': a break that cannot be a simple inversion of perspective (knowing how others see us). Looking instead of knowing how we look at others can be very instructive, but it is not enough to get rid of our 'orientalisms'); rather, it must consist of an ability to glimpse in others an autonomous and original perspective of universalization. The problems of the current Babel do not deal with how the so-called 'cultural differences' look at each other – in the reflexive and reciprocal double sense – but with how each one imagines and thinks the universal. What's more, not only as she imagines and thinks it, but also as she has collectively transcribed and codified it in her value statements, and in her declarations of principles and universal rights. As regards Europe's position on the new world scene, I would like to underline two aspects that I consider to be decisive. In the first place, we must never forget that Europe was both the land of revolutions and of the civilization of law and the continent of wars: it was from the heart of Europe, from the 'heart of darkness' of Europe, from which the wars of religion, the civil wars, and the two world wars were born with the horrors they provoked.

Secondly, we must not lose sight of the fact that Europe's wealth lies precisely in its differences.

Intersectionality: Universalism of Difference and the Politics of Translation

The unity of Europe was not founded on an ethnic, religious, linguistic, economic, or political unification, nor on an imaginary, mythological, psychosocial, or aesthetic unification but precisely on diversity and discontinuity. In this sense, Umberto Eco's affirmation that the language of Europe is translation has a symbolic charge that can be projected onto the polycentric scenario of planetary civilizations, redefining the meaning of legal and political universalism in radically new terms. In terms, that is, of what in my books of recent years I have called 'universalism of difference': adopting a philosophical lexicon, we could say that *difference – not identity – is the ontological texture of the universal.*

A universal that, in the multipolar world of our present, coincides with the idea of translation as a political project. The future of humanity depends entirely on the ability of the different civilizational contexts to translate each other, in an attempt to reach an agreement on certain key notions such as 'humanity', 'dignity', 'right', 'justice', 'freedom', and 'equality': decisive but highly controversial values, as was evident in the confrontation between Western and Asian representatives in the preparatory commissions for the Universal Declaration of Human Rights in 1948. We must increasingly try to translate the different meanings that the different languages and civilizations attribute to these terms-concepts, fundamental for the future of humanity on the planet.

But, at the same time, with the lucid awareness that something essential will always remain in the translation ... 'lost in translation'. And yet, the categorical imperative of the universalism of difference, in the face of an identity cosmopolitanism imposed on all other cultures by the hegemonic civilization of the West, forces us to try again and again to translate the principles and values of many cultural forms. In the firm conviction that the House of the Universal has not already been built once and for all by Westerners, that in this way we would welcome all the rest in our legally democratic civilization with more or less benevolent tolerance.

On the contrary – as the great philosopher, theologian, and writer of Spanish and Indian culture Raimon Panikkar, whom I had the privilege of knowing personally, has already warned – that house of the universal must always be rebuilt multilaterally.

Only in this perspective could a sovereign Europe play an important role in the new world scenario polarized by the new dualism between the United States and China and by the Cyber-Leviathan of the Internet and Artificial Intelligence. But this would require a grand political design from which the elites currently ruling the European Union appear light-years away.

Herein lies the paradox of our time: the continent that generated the concept of politics – starting from the classical Greek polis, to move on to the Roman idea of civitas and the modern concept of State, derived from the Latin expression *status reipublicae* and introduced for the first time by Machiavelli in the famous incipit of the Prince ('All States, all powers, that have held and hold rule over men have been and are either republics or principalities'.) – this same continent, that is Europe, appears at this moment as the subject weakest and politically most impotent on the new world stage.

In this time of interregnum we must therefore commit ourselves to writing the word 'universal' with one hand, and the word 'difference' with the other, resisting the temptation to write both words with a single, exclusive hand.

Because it would, however, be the wrong hand.

Afterword
Hayden White

Taking History Seriously

Commentary on Marramao's Philosophy of the Present

> *It is a daunting task, certainly, to try to grasp the intrinsic character of the present: to identify its logic and structure beyond the hubbub of contemporary events and to conceptualise this logic and structure in an adequate and appropriate fashion.*[1]

The present presents a particularly difficult problem for the historian because, although the present belongs to history quite as much as the past, the present cannot be studied adequately with the same instruments and methods used to study the past. This is because the present is not 'over and done with' but still in process of becoming; so we cannot, as we do with past events, claim to know how things have 'come out' as we claim to know about discrete series of events in the past. Of course, we can discern trends and movements and the dominant ones can be studied as indicators of a future that will someday look back to our present as its past. But we are not even clear about when the present begins and when, if ever, it might suddenly split apart, with some things suddenly becoming 'past' and other things suddenly arriving new as if from a 'future'. So, yes, indeed, as Marramao says, 'the logic and structure' of the present remain difficult to 'conceptualize'.

The 'logic and structure' of an age, an epoch, or any period of history constitute rather more a philosophical than a historiographical problem. This is because historians do not in general believe in the reality of the period; period designations such as 'the Renaissance', 'the Enlightenment', and even 'Paleo-Christian' are treated as conventional short-hand devices for indicating clusters of features of a given time span that distinguish it from other times. There is no substance or essence of, say, 'renascence' shared by all of the various revivals of classical antiquity from Carolingian times through the twelfth-century down to fifteenth-century Florence that license the use of the term 'renaissance' for all of them collectively. Nonetheless, rebirth and revival, renovation and reformation, and recovery and recall are all characteristic of specifically *historical* ways of thinking. Human beings' attempts to investigate the past in order to revive certain aspects of it as models of comportment, thought, and action are – or are thought to be – uniquely human ways of endowing a present with the spiritual resources by which to imagine a future for creative development, rather than a twilight heralding an end, death, and dissolution.

In *The Passage West*, Giacomo Marramao addresses issues such as these, not in an abstract manner but rather in terms of our present age grasped as a period of 'globalization'. Globalization is conventionally conceived as a *conflict* between those technological, financial, and political forces that have attained a worldwide scope of activity, and those 'local', 'regional', or even 'neighbourhood' niches where unique culture configurations have arisen. These local cultural niches are taken to manifest the diversity of human capabilities and they are thought to be threatened by the homogenizing processes of globalization, which require that everything be uniform, exchangeable, and standardized for their proper functioning. But Marramao does not see it this way. For him globalization is a stage on the way to a more comprehensive process of *universalization*, a process which has informed the expansive drive of all the great civilizations since the so-called 'Axial Age' but has been especially pronounced in Western civilization since the fusion of Christian missionarianism with Roman imperialism in late antiquity.

One reason for the many different interpretations of globalization ('clash of civilizations', 'end of history', and 'postmodernism') derives from the tendency of Western thinkers especially to conceptualize historical forces in antithetical (polar or oppositional) terms. Polarization, opposition, dichotomy, mutual exclusion, and a number of other logical tropes (such as identity and non-contradiction) seem to be a function of thinking in concepts or of conceptualization in general.

Marramao is not against concept-thinking *per se*, since it is difficult to even imagine scientific thinking without concepts. But unlike existent things, their processes and the relationships that obtain among things, concepts can represent thing-relations only in the logical modes of opposition, negation, negation of negation, and implication, whereas the relationships that obtain among incarnate things and processes are constituted primarily by *difference(s)*. And this is where Marramao swerves away from his earlier mentors Adorno and Habermas and towards such post-structuralist gurus as Foucault, Derrida, and Deleuze. These latter allow him to see a reality not comprised of antithetical opposites working towards a synthesis in which one of the terms succeeds in assimilating the other, but a world of differences working towards a structure of plurality, hybridity, and multiplicity in which all of the older modes of community – from clan to Nation State – are transcended and a post-Statist polity becomes possible.

So there is a decidedly utopian element in Marramao's vision of the possible futures that await us beyond globalization, but his is not a messianic or apocalyptical utopianism. It is simply a vision of what can be imagined as a possible future if we heed what *history* (not philosophy of history) has to tell us about the human condition of these, our times.[2] In this respect, Marramao's work is very much of a postmodernist nature: he rejects all of the 'grand narratives' of the past and offers instead, not a 'philosophy of history' as, rather, a 'philosophical' consideration of 'the history of the present'. Whence the relevance of the subtitle of his book, '*Philosophy* After the Age of the Nation State'. And the originality: there is a difference between a philosophy of history and a philosophical consideration of what professional historians would call 'the historical record'. Marramao does not pretend to be adding new data to the historical record; he proposes a new set of categories for the determination of what is new and original about the age of globalization, which follows upon the 'Age of the Nation State'. And the fundamental question has to be: Given the superannuation of the Nation State, what are the possible forms of polity that might follow upon it?

We who live in the 'our' present have a pretty good idea of what awaits us in our immediate future: a world in which certain undeniably *transnational* forces (communication, military, and surveillance technology, international markets and multinational financial corporations, migrational patterns, disease, and poverty) operate on a *global* plane, while various localities – from the farm and village, on the one hand, to the Nation State and certain interregional institutions such as the IMF, the World Bank, the European Union, the Chinese, Russian, and Indian blocs seek to manage or control these global forces and save something of those interests and institutions that endow discrete areas of the world with the charm of otherness.

For most of the world affected by its processes, globalization is a mixed blessing. Access to its benefits is limited, and avoidance of its effects is difficult and rare. But Marramao is doubtful as to whether we moderns fully comprehend what is really going on in globalization. For him globalization is for real, but it is less an end or goal of world civilization than, rather, a stage along the way to a realization of certain universal principles of sociality and selfhood. And although Marramao has a richly articulated array of examples to prove that homogenization and automatization are not inevitable consequences of globalization, much of his argument depends on his version of world history.

Now, the modern (post-Hegelian) philosophy of history is a product of an attempt to divine the universal meaning, purpose, aim, and goal of the world historical process by identifying the universal essence of historicity present in every local or regional history. As Ortega y Gassett said: 'Man has no nature. ... What he has is history' The 'secret' or inner meaning of *universal* history lies in the identification of what is specifically 'historical' in the different 'histories' studied by the 'historians' of the different cultures, civilizations, and nations of the world. Hegel's lectures on the topic are paradigmatic for this enterprise, while Marx, Comte, Spengler, and Toynbee represent variations in the direction of materialist and idealist metaphysics as the case might

be. But although it is obvious that the desire to synthesize the different histories of the nations of the world in order to identify their common 'historicist'
essence, this enterprise has been met with universal disregard and disdain by
both professional historians, on the one hand, and all manner of social scien-
tists and philosophers, on the other. Indeed, it is all but universally held that
the philosophy of history is a reworking of myth in pseudo-scientific terms
(Cassirer) and that the patterns discerned in world historical processes are little more than secularized versions of the great religious systems of antiquity.
In fact, in Lyotard's famous formulation, 'post-modernism' consists of little
else than the rejection of those 'grand narratives' of fate, destiny, progress,
redemption, eternal recurrence, and apocalypse in which the philosophy of
history has traded since its invention by St. Augustine in late antiquity.

For Marramao, the Nation State served as a solution to the problem of
Western civilizational identity caused by the dissolution of the *respublica
Christiana* and the secularization of Christian notions of the individual, society, and culture in modernity. But the Nation State has been rendered superannuated by globalization: global processes escape containment and regulation
by national institutions. This is why the present – our present age – requires
a radical reconceptualization of the fundamental problems of community and
society, to divine the 'logic and structure' of what is happening to us post-
moderns, and to imagine the form and content of the politics of a future, post-
global age.

The Passage West, Marramao tells us, 'is organized radially', like 'a theoretical map of the global', which, after a discussion of the difference between
our own age and everything preceding it, ends with 'the assertion of the thesis
of the passage to the Occident'. This 'passage' is not to be understood as
the worldwide adoption of Western institutions, values, aims, or goals but
rather the entrance into the post-national condition into which the Occident
has already passed as a result of its historical experience of exploration, colonization, imperialization, and capitalization, both of itself and of the rest of
the world. In other words, in our era the West has entered a phase in which,
because of globalization, it is so permeated by elements of other cultures that
it has lost most of those aspects of itself that have historically defined it.

This radial 'map', we are then told, will be filled out by the analyses of a
number of 'thematic epicentres' each comprised of a set of conceptual dyads:
'identity/difference, politics/law, sovereignty/global era, gift/exchange,
democracy/community, tolerance/recognition, and Europe/post-national public sphere' (xv). This circumnavigation is intended to aggregate into a kind
of collage expressive of a certain kind of 'cosmopolitan perspective', which
'must now pass through a radical redefinition of the universal: we need a
universal dimension setting out from the criterion of difference' (xii). This
in turn will allow 'a diametrical reversal' of a perspective that presupposes
'a disenchantment with politics and a mythologizing of identity'and lead to a
'demythologizing [of] identity' and a 're-enchanting [of] politics' (xiii).

What *is* the proper relation between the community and the individual, the citizen and the State, the particular and the universal, the thing and its species, or, summarily, the part and the whole of anything whatsoever? Absolutist regimes solved such problems by establishing hierarchies of power, rights, and duties on the basis of religious dogmas (*respublica Christiana*) or metaphysical propositions ('Leviathan') that assured continuity in change and identity even in contradiction. Paradoxes or contradictions in such systems (How can I be both a free person and an obedient subject?) were dealt with by the provision of certain myths which endowed contradiction itself with the aura of 'paradox', such as identity both individual and collective is both stable and changing; politics is both violent and redemptive; or economics is both rational and unpredictable. Such myths have received endorsement and legitimation by modern social sciences, as in Weber's notion of a natural affinity between 'the Protestant Ethic' and 'the Spirit of Capitalism'.

Moreover, such myths were also justified by the *modern* version of 'history', which purported to demonstrate that private vices can – paradoxically – result in public good (the 'hidden hand' doctrine), that violence and evil can result in progress and enlightenment (the 'progress' doctrine), and that time itself heals all wounds (the 'dialectic' doctrine). These myths are all, in Marramao's estimation, secular versions of earlier religious beliefs which, under the critique of modern materialistic science and certain historical events (imperialism and totalitarianism), have been *demystified*, leaving Western civilization with few resources to deal with the threats to world culture and society posed by post–Second World War 'globalization'.

The questions are fundamental to the global situation because global politics, economics, communications networks, electronic technology, and above all modern financial corporations transcend the limits of merely national societies and escape regulation by local laws and authorities. This is especially true of financial corporations that have become rogue entities grounded in no particular place on earth and answerable only to those laws that favour their own drive for profit. If they are not to descend into total anarchy the global market and financial system require a global polity, which, in turn, require a global legal system. The traditional human sciences do not possess the categories and methods to do anything more than disclose the anomalies of the fundamental principles of post-nation state institutions and practices, for example, conflicts between law and morality, between politics and ethics, worth and value in exchange, between authority and power in politics, and so on. As long as the Nation State retained its mystique as manifestation of a land–language–people complex sacred in nature and worthy of a devotion equal to that of the Church or Monarchy, such anomalies could be taken on faith as divine mysteries, like the Trinity or the Incarnation, cleansing and redemptive precisely by virtue of their transcendence of the powers of human understanding.

Western philosophy since Plato down to Heidegger has typically confused things with concepts and has thereby locked itself into endless debate
over how to synthesize things which, identified by their concepts, can never
achieve identity with one another. This is why, until philosophy comes to
terms with its greatest postmodern critics – Heidegger, Foucault, Derrida,
Deleuze, Rorty, Agamben, Adorno, Badiou, and so on – it will remain indentured to servitude to the anomalous idea of the 'coincidence of opposites',
more of a figure than a concept and thus alien from philosophy until philosophy itself becomes liberated from the fetishism of the concept. This is part of
the message of postmodernist philosophizing (or anti-philosophizing) which,
however, fails in its own way by its denial of the adequacy of a post-identi-
tarian logic to a world inhabited by individuals who are themselves caught
between the aridity of the concept and the living reality of the figure.

But if philosophy is to deal with such matters, it has itself to get over or
transcend an anomaly of its own, namely, the challenge to its traditional form
presented by certain late modern, seemingly anti-traditional, sects such as
phenomenology, existentialism, pragmatism, deconstruction, poststructural-
ism, feminism, postcolonialism, and so on, which, allegedly, threaten the very
substance of traditional philosophizing itself. Marramao sees this conflict
between the old and new modes of thinking as analogous to that between the
global and local itself. The anomalies generated by philosophy's traditional
manner of construing relations between its positive and negative valences can
be resolved by the abandonment of the relationship of opposition in favour of
some notion of what appear to be antithetical concepts as *mutually implica-
tive*. In the same way that globalism has at once frightened local regions of the
human ecumene with 'homologation', but at the same time resistance to such
homologation has strengthened awareness of the value of localities and have,
in certain locales, resulted in their strengthening, so too traditional philosophy may be strengthened by assimilating the postmodernist sectarians to their
own uses – and vice versa. The ways by and in which indigenous peoples and
local cultural groups have adapted techniques, practices, and values usually
associated with the global to the needs and interests of a local kind, is a theme
of much anthropological discussion these days.[3] But whether the local can
sustain itself against the solvent power of the global market or must suffer the
fate of commodification and exchange valorization only is an open question.
Marramao puts his bets neither on traditional philosophy nor its postmodernist avatar but rather on what Vico and modern pragmatists call a *praxis* armed
against abstract conceptualization, on the one hand, and warmed over tradition, on the other.

So too in politics: to see the one and the many as *opposed* in the way that
the concepts of good and evil, or negative and positive, might be related is to
bind oneself to the possibility of Hegelian synthesis or to unjustified judgement in favour of the one or the other (either/or thinking). Marramao is much
more inclined to a kind of Spinozist monism in which difference is primary,

and fundamental relationships are construed in a modalist manner as relations among differences. Such an approach to the problem of the relation between the global and the local allows him to abandon two impediments to a desirable pluralism in psychology and group dynamics, what he calls the myth of identity, on one hand, and a disenchanted politics, on the other. He thinks that the myth of identity (or self-sameness) and a politics based either on the idea of community or an obsession with the friend–foe dyad are both versions of the myth of 'sameness'. And he proceeds to deconstruct both the myth and the incarnation in ideas of individuality (both of the person and of the community or nation) and of the nation (both as the incarnation of the community, on the one side, and as ideal to be protected from the enemy, defined as anyone who differs from commune). The same kind of deconstruction is carried out on the dyad law/politics, in which the former is construed as the incarnation of the national ethos, on the one hand, and the latter, politics, is demonized as the very incarnation of power as *raison d'état*, devoid of all morality and of any responsibility to the law of the land, since the modern State is the one institution claiming the right to declare the (Schmittian) 'state of exception'.

In a brilliant chapter on Carl Schmitt's political and jurisprudential philosophy, Marramao finds a radical novelty in Schmitt's idea that sovereignty consists in the power to make, revise, or abrogate the law itself. The modern States seemingly exist to incarnate the national *ethnos*, administer the law within the confines of the nation, and protect the people from foreign enemies. But since politics presupposes that the difference between the inside of the community and its outside consists of the oppositional pair friend and enemy, it inevitably ends in times of stress by regarding the citizenry itself in the same terms. For Schmitt the modern corporate state, which claims sovereignty over the law itself, is the proper form of the state in modernity.

Modernity in this case means a situation in which religion has been disestablished or subordinated to the state, and 'nature' or any part of it has lost is status as *fons et origo* of both law and morality, and the *polis* has become *Leviathan* whether of the dictatorial or the communal kind. Under such conditions, the kind of 'Peace of Westphalia ideal' of autonomous nations negotiating settlements of disputes in service to a 'European' community's long-term interests, is no longer viable as a model for global or regional unities, especially in areas where those unities are riven by ethnic, religious, and social differences. In other words, 'after the Nation State' means that the nation itself is no longer a viable unit for the organization of global economic and communicational systems.

Reflecting on this circumstance, Marramao switches from a horizontal to a vertical model of organization and proposes instead a system of combination on different levels of organization, from the micro-level of the family and farm all the way up to the high-tech communications and financial networks where everything is homologous and value is tied to nothing of a local provenance. In sum, Marramao, at least in this book in a chapter entitled 'Europe after the

Leviathan', which was originally published in 2001, which is to say, before the crash of 2008, recommends the European Union as a kind of 'Federalist' system which serve as a model for a global political–legal structure adequate to the needs of a global financial and communications network. Marramao thinks that globalization has the capacity for both the homologation and the diversification of human culture and society. Contemporary globalization differs from its earlier avatars (attempts at unifications of parts of the world by conquest, trade, technology, political and economic institutions, cultural borrowing, missionary activity, exploration, colonization, and the like) by virtue of its origin in *difference*.[4]

By 'philosophy' we usually mean that brand of Western European thinking intimately linked to not only modern physical sciences but also the more general world view that comes into play with the establishment of the modern Western European nation state, with its idea of a *genius populi* providing a substance shared by individual citizens who, in pursuing their own 'enlightened'self-interests, providentially succeed in 'realizing' the universal destiny of the human race. It has been the unique function of philosophy to serve as the rational and realistic *organon* of humanity's effort to realize its destiny, both at home (in the European 'community' of nations) and abroad in the ecumene perceivable as emerging within the process known as globalization. For Marramao, the other human sciences must fail to grasp the essence of this new phenomenon, prone as they are to treating the relation between political authority and the multitude in either reductively mechanistic or inflationary transcendental terms. Even philosophy itself was hindered from coming to terms with the contradictions inherent in Western notions of community as long as it remained indentured to the Nation State model of society and the quantitative methods of the physical science as its epistemic model. But now that the establishment of worldwide networks of communications, politics, and finance has rendered the *Nation* State, along with all other merely regional or local polities superannuated, both philosophy and politics have been liberated from their former condition of subordination to the Nation's cultural, ethical, epistemic, and ethnic presuppositions. And therewith both philosophy and politics are freed to engage and exploit the new perspectives on world history provided by globalization. And Marramao's project can suddenly be seen as a redemption of the idea of globalization by the philosophical demonstration that globalization is itself the solution to the problems created by its own appearance on the world scene.

Notes

1   The essay by Hayden White reproduced in this appendix (and published in 2015 in a Special Issue of 'Politica Común' dedicated to my work) addresses some crucial themes of my philosophical–political approach to the question of the present, starting from my book *The Passage West: Philosophy After the Age of the Nation State*, Verso, London,New York 2012, whose themes are developed and updated precisely

in *Towards a New Concept of the Political*. Hayden sadly left us on March 5, 2018. I therefore intend to dedicate this book to him: to his memory, to his generous friendship.

2 Speaking of 'these, our times', see Marramao (2007), a study of what we might call 'qualitative' time – the time of judgement and decision, the time of action and self-determination in human life – as against the purely 'quantitative' time of equal units, regular process, and finitude. Also see Andrew Baird's review.

3 See Clifford.

4 Marramao uses the term 'difference' in much the same way Derrida uses the French neologism 'différance'. For Derrida the latter names a condition ontologically prior to the distinction between active and passive modes of being. For Marramao, difference names a condition prior to the formation of notions of identity and the One, both of which he regards as myths embedded surreptitiously in the heart of post-Socratic philosophy in the West. What all of that expansion over the globe undertaken by the West since the Crusades revealed was the impossibility of identity and the delusional nature of the One. Contemporary globalization is less interested in conquering, colonizing, and exploiting local sites of traditional practices of cultural and economic production than in subsuming them to the exigencies of exchange as an end in itself. Globalization effects flows of goods, information, persons, institutions, and so on, in many directions: from the metropolitan centres out to the periphery and vice versa, thereby effecting changes in the localities in the periphery, but also vice versa, as the former colonists make their way to the metropolitan centres (Turks to Germany, Poles to Ireland, Somalis to Italy, Indians to the UK, etc.), changing the cultures of these centres radically.

Works Referenced

Baird, Andrew. "History and *Kairós*". In *History and Theory*, 50 (2011): 120–128.

Clifford, James. *Returns: Becoming Indigenous in the Modern World*. Cambridge, Harvard UP, 2014.

Marramao, Giacomo. *Kairós: Towards an Ontology of 'Due Time'*. Aurora, The Davies Group, 2007.

———. *The Passage West: Philosophy After the Age of the Nation State*. Translated by Matteo Mandarini. Afterword by Antonio Negri. London-New York, Verso, 2012.

Index

For Product Safety Concerns and Information please contact our EU
representative GPSR@taylorandfrancis.com
Taylor & Francis Verlag GmbH, Kaufingerstraße 24, 80331 München, Germany